To SUE,

ENJOY!

THOMAS
CURTIS

WHIPPED & CHARRED

Whipped & Charred

By Thomas Curtis

©2017 Meze Publishing

All rights reserved.

First edition printed in 2017 in the UK.

ISBN: 978-1-910863-20-6

Written by: Rachel Heward

Edited by: Phil Turner

Photography by: Marc Barker

Designed by: Paul Cocker, Marc Barker
and Matt Crowder

PR: Kerre Chen

Contributors: Sarah Gunton

Published by Meze Publishing Limited

Unit 1B

2 Kelham Square

Kelham Riverside

Sheffield

S3 8SD

Web: www.mezepublishing.co.uk

Tel: 0114 275 7709

Email: info@mezepublishing.co.uk

Printed by Bell and Bain Ltd, Glasgow

Contents

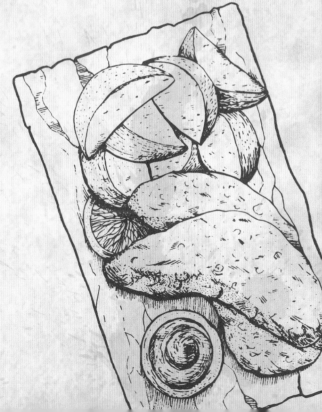

I HAVE ALWAYS BEEN DRAWN TO COOKING;

From a young age I remember being fascinated by the way in which my grandmother, known to me as "Mama", measured out the ingredients to make scones. It was almost a science, approached like an experiment – with very tasty results. She was the home-cook of the family, but my mother has always worked in the industry in some form or another, so I grew up in the pub business. I would go with her to open up the pub on cold mornings, and tuck into things like ham, egg and chips, or a meat and potato pie for my dinner. Cooked from scratch, it was pub grub done properly, unlike the bought-in stuff that you often find knocking around these days.

The family has strong ties to The White Hart in Minster Lovell in particular. Around twelve years ago my mum, Mandy, and step dad, Brian, used to run it. So it was here that, as a fifteen year old on a work experience placement, I found myself up to my elbows in dirty pots or a huge pile of potato peelings. After a hiatus, my mum and Brian returned to the pub that had been left in a state of almost disrepair, and I was appointed as head chef. It needed a lot of work – the restaurant itself was just a dusky room with an old pool table and the kitchen needed a major facelift. However the opportunity was just too good to resist; who would have thought that I would one day be running the first professional kitchen I'd ever set foot in?

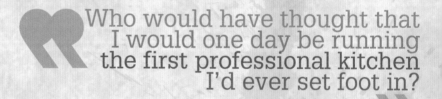

Who would have thought that I would one day be running the first professional kitchen I'd ever set foot in?

Introduction

It was never actually a career path I'd intended, it was only when leaving school at sixteen that the reality of needing a job dawned on me, and cooking was the one thing I was truly passionate about. Obsessed with TV shows like MasterChef, and an ardent fan of the likes of Anthony Bourdain and Marco Pierre White (I even have a tattoo of the latter on my leg) I decided to give it a go. Of course, knowing the industry and all of its pitfalls well, my mother tried to discourage me via the purchase of Bourdain's brutally honest book, Kitchen Confidential, not knowing this would be more inspiring to me than scaremongering. Passionate and ruthless, the chefs I was reading about and watching were taking things to the next level and it made me want to be a part of their world.

I started at The New Inn, now known as The Dovecote, in a part-time role. This was my first proper job and I was unbelievably nervous, but took to my task of preparing the salads and a few other cold dishes quickly. My enthusiasm clearly paid off as within just one month I was offered a full-time position and I never looked back. It was here that I worked with two great people, Mat Tucker and Richard Lenik, who taught me a lot about temperament in the kitchen. When you see the kitchens on TV all guns blazing, chefs swearing and saucepans flying across the room, you imagine that's just how it is, and how it's supposed to be. But at The New Inn, I discovered you produce the best food when the atmosphere is calm and cooperative. I saw Mat as a bit of a father figure as well as a great friend, so I followed him to The Lamb at Crawley to continue my culinary education.

At the The Lamb, it was all about good, honest food like slow roasts and creamed mushrooms with garlic; things that may be considered a bit old school, but it was executed superbly. It was the perfect environment to master the basics and take on extra responsibility as a chef.

After my time was up at The Lamb, I bounced around a few places but never felt settled until I rejoined Richard at Hackett's in Witney. I was here for around four to five years, during which time we encouraged each other creatively; we both had a similar style of cooking, which meant we brought the best out in each other. I've always considered it an utter privilege to work with that man.

Cooking was the one thing I was truly passionate about.

The kind of food that I'm interested in creating has always been hearty, classic. There's something about home comforts that makes me happy. I could have gone down the Michelin route but the level that those guys are at is astonishing; it takes an awful lot of sacrifice. Besides, I love visiting fine-dining restaurants like The Fat Duck and Restaurant Gordon Ramsay, and if I worked in that environment I think it would lose the magic.

I have so much freedom at The White Hart to create what I want and it's been a huge learning curve discovering what works and what doesn't. There's something satisfying about coming up with a dish and seeing it succeed, or even fail; if anything you gain more from making a few mistakes. There were 15 menu changes in the first 18 months we took over, and that's both because we were finding our feet, and because we like to roll with the seasons and keep things fresh. We also had to start small as I was literally a one man band – doing everything from the prep through to the washing up. Now I have a great team behind me and we've developed the menu to include everything from your simple pub classics like steak and Guinness pie, to slightly more elegant dishes like Asian spiced belly pork, or wild mushroom and truffle cannelloni.

There's something about home comforts that makes me happy.

The same ethos runs throughout; the ingredients are fresh, seasonal and locally sourced. Our vegetables and micro-herbs are sourced from Oxfordshire and most of our meat is from Baker's Butchers in Witney, who source everything within a five mile radius of the shop itself. Warner's Butchers are another brilliant local supplier, delivering exceptional quality week in week out. The meat we get in for our roasts is of such a great quality that Sundays get booked up four weeks in advance! I've put this success down to consistency – serving belly pork, breast of lamb and topside of beef, we strive to make sure the pork always has crackling, the lamb is succulent and tender, and the beef is perfectly cooked and pink in the middle. And then there's the proper gravy of course…

To give something back, we offer a 'produce for a pint scheme' whereby people trade their home-grown fruit and veg for a nice cold beer. It's an agreeable trade-off, and a great way to get people involved, though one time we were stuck with four kilos of Jerusalem artichoke! The community is at the heart of this place and we couldn't do it without local trade from Minster Lovell and Witney. Nearby hotels are also incredibly supportive, sending tourists up our way if they ask for recommendations. I am delighted that since we opened we have been awarded 'Best Traditional Pub' in the Oxfordshire Food & Drink Awards, made appearances on Oxford TV and Radio Oxford, plus we represented the county in the Oxfordshire Cook Book. A combination of passionate staff and loyal customers has made this happen, and I can't wait to continue this journey with them.

Introduction

There are a few reasons why I wanted to do this book. Firstly, a bit of a selfish one is that it's a personal dream of mine, and I think any chef would be lying if they said they didn't want their own cook book! Secondly, it's a tribute to my late father. He was as passionate as me about my dream, and I think seeing this book in print would have made him very proud. Finally, this is my chance to give something back to all of the people who have supported me. It's for my friends and family – I hope they enjoy and cherish these recipes as much as I've enjoyed putting them together.

This book is not about flash food and everyone from beginners to experts will be able to give these recipes a go. They are tried and tested and I've done my best to create a diverse range of dishes, from light bites to seafood, vegetarian options, meat dishes, suppers, sides and sweets, I've covered pretty much all bases, including how to make things like staple sauces – and I've even thrown in a couple of cocktails!

 ## Any chef would be lying if they said they didn't want their own cook book! 〝〝

You don't need any specialist equipment either, just a decent non-stick pan, and a food processor would probably come in handy. My advice for any of the recipes would be to keep an open mind, and if there's something you want to change then go ahead and do it! Add, take away or amend as you wish. Recipes are great as guidelines, for enhancing your knowledge of flavour profiles, to be used for ideas and gaining inspiration for your own creations. You don't have to necessarily do things by the book. That's why I've created the seasonality chart and flavour wheel on page 14. I want to get you thinking about food combinations – a good rule I've always kept in mind is to see how things are paired in nature. For example, deer and lamb eat berries and grass, and mushrooms often grow near woody herbs. Get creative with it!

Finally, I'd urge you to shop local. Chat to your butcher as they're in the best position to source almost anything you might want, and they'll often help you with cooking tips like timings too. Greengrocers and farm shops are undoubtedly the best for shopping organic and keeping the food miles down, plus they're usually a lot cheaper than supermarket alternatives.

I hope you'll have fun exploring the recipes of this book, shopping for the best ingredients, experimenting with flavours and creating some tasty dishes that you can share with your nearest and dearest. Bon appétit!

SEASONALITY CHART

SPRING

FORCED RHUBARB gooseberries APRICOTS cauliflower
ARTICHOKES asparagus CELERY wild garlic SPRING GREENS
chicory JERSEY ROYALS leeks sprouting broccoli PEAS spinach BROAD
BEANS leeks SPRING ONIONS spinach CHIVES chervil
OREGANO tarragon THYME dill BAY parsley
BASIL rosemary CORIANDER mackerel
POLLOCK crab SCALLOPS sardine SEA BASS
spring lamb hogget SPRING
CHICKEN

SUMMER

cherries PEACH plums BANANAS
APRICOTS melons PLUMS redcurrant WATERMELON peach
greengages FIGS nectarines strawberries grapes RADISHES
kohlrabi PEAS broad beans DAMSONS samphire BLACKBERRIES
chard FENNEL courgette GARLIC sweetcorn
AUBERGINE asparagus MARROW marjoram
MINT basil SORREL halibut TOMATOES HADDOCK
whiting COLEY salmon
SEA BASS tuna VEAL

AUTUMN

nectarines CLEMENTINES SWEDE celery
blueberries nectarines truffles COURGETTE CARROTS
SQUASH truffles CHESTNUTS turnips
parsnips KALE peppers artichokes sprouts turnips
CELERIAC jerusalem artichokes CHESTNUTS coley MACKEREL
CABBAGES thyme SAGE OYSTERS coley pheasant
wild mushrooms PUMPKIN brussel sardine GUINEA FOWL
figs ELDERBERRIES aubergine SQUASH venison PARTRIDGE
cranberries APPLE quince QUINCE

WINTER

DATES clementines BLOOD
pomegranate clementines ORANGES grapefruit CRANBERRIES
HISPI CABBAGE savoy cabbage radicchio SQUASH CAULIFLOWER BUTTERNUT
chicory WATERCRESS swede sweet potato SALSIFY onions PAK CHOI
BAY turnips KALE rosemary SAGE CAVOLO NERO SPINACH
SOLE oysters SEA BASS mussels haddock
goose TURKEY pork GROUSE DUCK
beef

WEIGHTS AND MEASURES CONVERSION TABLE

TEMPERATURES

110°c	90°c (fan)	225°f	Gas ¼
120°c	100°c (fan)	250°f	
130°c	110°c (fan)	260°f	Gas ½
140°c	120°c (fan)	275°f	Gas 1
150°c	130°c (fan)	300°f	Gas 2
160°c	140°c (fan)	315°f	
170°c	150°c (fan)	325°f	Gas 3
180°c	160°c (fan)	350°f	Gas 4
190°c	170°c (fan)	375°f	Gas 5
200°c	180°c (fan)	400°f	Gas 6
210°c	190°c (fan)	415°f	
220°c	200°c (fan)	425°f	Gas 7
230°c	210°c (fan)	450°f	Gas 8

VOLUME

5ml		1 teaspoon
10ml		1 dessertspoon
15ml	½fl oz	1 tablespoon
30ml	1fl oz	
55ml	2fl oz	
70ml	2½fl oz	
90ml	3½fl oz	
115ml	4fl oz	
130ml	4½fl oz	
140ml	5fl oz	¼ pint
155ml	5½fl oz	
170ml	6fl oz	
185ml	6½fl oz	
200ml	7fl oz	
225ml	8fl oz	
285ml	10fl oz	½ pint
400ml	14fl oz	
425ml	15fl oz	¾ pint
565ml	20fl oz	1 pint
710ml	25fl oz	1¼ pints
850ml	30fl oz	1½ pints
1 litre	35fl oz	1¾ pints

WEIGHT

10g	½oz
20g	¾oz
25g	1oz
50g	2oz
100g	3oz
150g	5oz
200g	6oz
250g	9oz
300g	10oz
400g	14oz
450g	1lb
500g	1lb 2oz

LIQUID & DRY EQUIVALENTS

2 tbsp	1fl oz	25ml	30g
1 cup	¼ quart	250ml	225g
2 cups	1 pint	500ml	450g
4 cups	35fl oz	1 litre	
4 quarts	1 gallon	3.75 litres	

Ounces to grams	multiply by 28.35
Teaspoons to millilitres	multiply by 5
Tablespoons to millilitres	multiply by 15
Fluid ounces to millilitres	multiply by 30
Cups to litres	multiply by 0.24

LENGTH

5mm	¼in
1cm	2/5in
2.5cm	1in
5cm	2in
10cm	4in
20cm	7¾in
50cm	1ft 7½in
1m	3ft 3½in

LIGHT BITES

Quick mid-week dinners, lunches, starters and snacks; this section covers it all, from herby sausage rolls (perfect for picnics) to warming cauliflower, sage and buttermilk soup. Simple food can be inspiring too!

Beef carpaccio with toasted hazelnuts

Preparation time: 10 minutes | Serves 6-8 | gluten-free | dairy-free

It is essential to get the best quality fillet steak you can for this, and I urge you to use your local butcher to make this happen. You will not be disappointed.

500g top quality beef fillet steak

50g hazelnuts, chopped and toasted

1 orange, zest

50g rocket leaves

Olive oil

Sea salt

Freshly ground black pepper

Using a very sharp knife, slice the fillet steak into 2mm thin slices.

Place these slices in between two bits of cling film and gently bash with a rolling pin until they are wafer thin.

Continue this process until all of the fillet steak has been prepared, then fan them out on a large flat board or plate.

Scatter the carpaccio with the hazelnuts, orange zest and rocket leaves and then drizzle generously with olive oil.

Finally, season to taste with sea salt and freshly ground black pepper.

This dish is perfect on its own but is also great paired with a good loaf of crusty bread.

Blue cheese bon bons with apple and thyme dipping sauce

Preparation time: 20 minutes | Cooking time: 5 minutes | Serves 4

A nod in the direction of a classic cheese and biscuits plate; perfect for the end of a dinner party.

1 large cooking apple, peeled and diced	Salt and pepper
2 sprigs of thyme, leaves stripped from stalk	30g flat leaf parsley, finely chopped
2 tbsp cider vinegar	500g good quality blue cheese
4 tbsp caster sugar	1 egg yolk
2 shallots, finely diced	400g fresh breadcrumbs
1 celery stick, finely diced	3 whole eggs, beaten
Olive oil	100g plain flour

In a saucepan add the diced apple, thyme, cider vinegar and caster sugar. Cover it up and cook over a medium heat for 10-15 minutes until the apples are very soft. Check every few minutes to make sure it doesn't catch and burn. If it looks too dry, add a splash of water.

Transfer this mix to a food processor and blend until smooth. Alternatively you can use a potato masher to work until smooth.

In a frying pan sauté the shallots and celery with a drizzle of olive oil over a medium heat for 6 minutes until soft and translucent. Season with a good pinch of salt and pepper and transfer to a mixing bowl. Allow to cool completely.

Add the parsley, blue cheese, egg yolk and 200g of breadcrumbs to the shallots and celery. Mix thoroughly and roll into small bite sized balls. Lay on a plate or baking tray and chill for 1 hour to firm up.

Preheat a deep fat fryer to 180°c or place enough oil in a wok or large saucepan to come halfway up the pan.

Place over a medium heat and to test whether it's hot enough drop a cube of bread into the oil. It will be hot enough when the bread fries to a golden colour.

Take each ball and dip first in to the flour, then in the beaten egg and finally the breadcrumbs. Repeat this process twice with each ball to get a good coating.

Gently fry in batches for 2-3 minutes until golden brown. Season with salt and pepper and serve immediately with the apple dipping sauce.

Bubble and squeak

Preparation time: 5 minutes | Cooking time: 20 minutes | Serves 4

Near enough anything can be put into a great bubble and squeak, so it was pretty hard to put together a definitive ingredients list! Traditionally it is a dish created from the leftovers of a previous meal; as the most common is a Sunday roast, I've stuck to that formula with some cooked veg and roast potatoes.

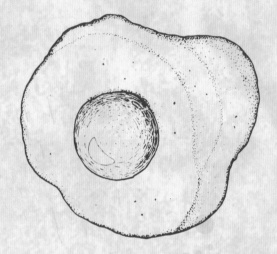

6 cooked roast potatoes

2 cooked carrots

1 cooked parsnip

100g cooked red cabbage

50g garden peas

6 florets cooked broccoli

2 sprigs thyme

Salt and pepper

Vegetable oil, beef dripping or goose fat

Preheat the oven to 220°c/200°c fan.

Simply chop all of the ingredients into equal sized pieces and place into a large mixing bowl. Strip the leaves from the thyme and add to the vegetables. Season well with salt and pepper. Using your hands or a potato masher, bring everything together well.

Heat up a large cast iron skillet over a medium/high heat with either a good swig of vegetable oil or a tablespoon of beef dripping or goose fat.

Carefully place the bubble and squeak mixture into the hot fat and push to the edges using a spoon.

Place into the oven on the middle shelf and cook for around 15-20 minutes.

Remove from the oven and allow to stand for a couple of minutes. The bottom should be crispy and golden brown. Spoon onto plates and serve. I like to have mine with a runny fried egg and fried spam. Delicious.

Cauliflower, sage and buttermilk soup

Preparation time: 10 minutes | Cooking time: 30 minutes | Serves 6-8 | gluten-free

This beautiful creamy soup is taken to the next level with the use of rich buttermilk; an underused ingredient that can be found in most good supermarkets.

2 tbsp olive oil

Salt and pepper

1 cauliflower

50g unsalted butter

1 shallot, diced

1 potato, diced

1 stick of celery, diced

4 cloves of garlic, diced

500ml buttermilk

250ml double cream

250ml vegetable stock

10 large sage leaves, removed from stalk

Preheat the oven to 190°c/170°c fan. Bring a pan of water to the boil and add 2 tablespoons of salt.

Remove the cauliflower from its leaves and cut off the florets, keeping the stalk. Blanch the florets in boiling water for 2 minutes then drain in a colander.

Place the blanched florets on a baking tray with the butter, cover with foil and bake for 20 minutes in the preheated oven.

Heat up the olive oil in a heavy based saucepan and add the shallot, potato, celery and garlic.

Finely dice the cauliflower stalk that you kept and add this to the saucepan.

Turn the heat to medium and stir well until everything softens and caramelises.

Add in the buttermilk, double cream, vegetable stock and sage.

Remove the cauliflower from the oven and add this to the saucepan. Bring everything to a simmer and cook on a medium heat for another 15 minutes.

Remove from the heat and blend in a food processor or use a hand blender until silky smooth.

Serve immediately with sage leaf to garnish.

Confit chicken salad with ginger and honey dressing

Preparation time: 10 minutes | Cooking time: 4 hours | Serves 6 | gluten-free

A versatile dish that is just as good in the winter as it is the summer. Feel free to add other ingredients to perk it up, such as fresh red chilli or anchovies.

6 chicken legs

Salt and pepper

4 garlic cloves, crushed

Sprig of thyme

6 bay leaves

600ml vegetable oil

3 red onions

50g fresh ginger

3 tsp clear honey

3 tsp Dijon mustard

3 tsp white wine vinegar

100ml olive oil (plus a little bit extra for drizzling)

3 baby gem lettuce

1 buffalo mozzarella ball

Toasted pine nuts

Preheat the oven to 180°c/160°c fan.

Place the chicken legs into a deep baking tray and season generously with salt and pepper.

Add the garlic cloves, thyme and bay leaves to the chicken and pour over all of the vegetable oil.

Cover with foil and place on the bottom shelf of the oven and roast for 4 hours.

Peel the red onions and cut into quarters, spread evenly on a separate baking tray, drizzle with a little bit of the olive oil and season with salt and pepper.

Roast in the oven for the remaining 30 minutes of cooking time prior to the chicken legs coming out.

Remove the chicken legs and onions from the oven and allow to cool to room temperature. Separate the chicken legs from the oil and, along with the onions, place in the fridge to cool until ready to serve.

For the dressing, blend the ginger, honey, Dijon mustard and white wine vinegar in a food processor until smooth.

Strain any fibres out through a fine sieve into a mixing bowl and whisk in the olive oil at a slow and steady pace. The dressing should be glossy and smooth.

To assemble and serve, gently remove the leaves from the baby gem lettuce and wash thoroughly under a cold tap. Shake dry and place them within an individual serving bowl.

Remove the skin from the chicken legs and tear off the meat from the bone; allow this to fall onto the baby gem leaves.

Place the roasted red onion around the dish and tear off pieces of buffalo mozzarella to be arranged on the salad.

Finish with a scatter of toasted pine nuts and a generous lashing of the ginger and honey dressing.

Herby sausage rolls
with Marie Rose sauce

Preparation time: 15 minutes | Cooking time: 25 minutes | Makes 6 sausage rolls

A classic and a staple for lunch boxes up and down the country, these sausage rolls take advantage of the wonderful herbs we have available to us at most times during the year.

2 tsp olive oil

4 shallots, finely diced

900g pork sausage meat

20g flat leaf parsley, chopped

10g sage, chopped

10g rosemary, chopped

10g thyme, stripped from stem

1 orange, zest

Salt and pepper

320g pre-rolled puff pastry

3 egg yolks, for glazing

4 tbsp mayonnaise

1 tbsp tomato ketchup

1 tsp horseradish sauce

1 tsp Worcestershire sauce

1 tsp tabasco sauce

Preheat an oven to 180°c/160°c fan.

Heat a teaspoon of olive oil in a frying pan and sauté the diced shallots until caramelised and golden in colour, and allow to cool.

In a mixing bowl combine the pork sausage meat, flat leaf parsley, sage, rosemary, thyme and orange zest.

Season well with salt and pepper.

Roll out the puff pastry sheet and cut into six even rectangles.

Divide the sausage mixture between the puff pastry portions.

Mix together the egg yolks and remaining teaspoon of olive oil and glaze around the sausage meat, coating the puff pastry.

Roll up one side of the puff pastry and fold it back under itself.

Place each sausage roll seam side down on a baking tray lined with greaseproof paper.

Glaze the tops of the sausage rolls with the egg mixture, sprinkle with salt and pepper, then score the tops with the back of a knife.

Bake in the preheated oven for 25 minutes on the bottom shelf until golden brown.

Remove and allow to cool while you make the Marie Rose sauce.

In a bowl, mix together the mayonnaise, tomato ketchup, horseradish, Worcestershire sauce and tabasco.

Serve the warm sausage rolls with a generous dollop of the Marie Rose sauce.

Heritage tomatoes with Parma ham and walnut pesto

Preparation time: 10 minutes | Serves 6 | dairy-free

In my eyes, this is a dish that can only be served in the height of summer. When tomatoes are so ripe they are fit to burst, there are fewer things on earth I'd rather eat. With the great varieties that are now readily available to us; it's time to show you a show stopping dish that is packed full of not only colour, but immense flavour as well.

100g parsley, chopped

100g walnuts, chopped

10ml sesame oil

100ml olive oil

2 cloves garlic, chopped

1 small lemon, juice and zest

700g mixed heritage tomatoes

Sea salt and freshly cracked black pepper

12 slices Parma ham

50g watercress

In a food processor, pulse together the parsley, walnuts, sesame oil, olive oil, garlic, lemon juice and zest until you have a chunky but well mixed dressing.

Cut the tomatoes into different shapes and sizes; vary it with halves, slices and chunks. Visually, anything will be impressive if the colours are bright and bold.

Divide the tomatoes between four bowls, sprinkle each with a little sea salt.

Place two bits of Parma ham onto each plate by pulling it apart and winding it through the tomatoes.

Generously spoon the walnut pesto over, top with a few sprigs of fresh watercress and a grinding of black pepper.

Welsh rarebit toastie with crispy bacon and maple syrup

Preparation time: 10 minutes | Cooking time: 30 minutes | Serves 4

There's a cheese toastie and then there's this cheese toastie. Pure decadence and completely gluttonous, this is such a treat and well worth the effort to impress. If you're just making it for yourself, make the same batch of rarebit and keep it in the fridge for up to 5 days. You can slice off what you want and put it on top of toast.

You'll need a good solid cast iron skillet or a large flat frying pan, also some baking parchment.

50g unsalted butter

50g plain flour

200ml full fat milk

50ml dark ale

100g strong cheddar cheese, grated

50g stilton, grated

1 tsp english mustard

1 tsp Worcestershire sauce

Chives, chopped

Salt and pepper

8 slices thick cut white bread

8 rashers streaky bacon

4 tsp maple syrup

In a heavy based saucepan, melt the butter over a medium heat and gradually whisk in the plain flour until you have a roux (this should be a thick, pale yellow paste). Pour the ale into the milk and whisk a quarter of this mix into the roux, whisking all the time.

Slowly add the remaining milk mixture until you have a silky smooth sauce.

Turn the heat down to low and whisk in the cheddar and stilton cheeses, as well as the English mustard and Worcestershire sauce, season with salt and pepper to taste. Continue to whisk until the cheeses have melted and you have a thick mixture. Line a shallow 20x20cm with cling film and pour in the rarebit mixture. Allow to cool and set in the fridge for 2 hours.

Heat your grill to a medium high heat and lay the streaky bacon and a tray lined with foil. Cook for 10 minutes, flipping the bacon over half way and draining the excess fat (save this).

Set the bacon aside, it should go really crispy as it cools slightly.

Brush your white bread with the bacon fat, this will be on the outside of the sandwich. Cut 8 squares of baking parchment a little bit larger than each slice of bread and place a slice of bread, fat side down, onto the parchment. Now begin to assemble the sandwich.

Remove the rarebit from the fridge and persuade it from the cling film. Cut into 4 squares and flatten slightly with your hands, place each square onto a piece of bread then lay over two rashers of your crispy bacon. Drizzle with maple syrup and season with a little more salt and pepper. Sandwich together with the other pieces of bread, fat side up.

Heat up a frying pan or skillet over a medium heat. Depending on how large the pan is, cook one or two toasties together. Place each one into the hot dry pan, the baking parchment will protect it from scorching the bread too much. Cook each one for around 3 minutes each side until golden brown and the rarebit should begin to ooze. If you feel the heat is too high, just lower it slightly and let the pan cool for a minute or two.

Serve straight from the pan, cut into big triangles. Great with a glass of ale!

SEAFOOD

Though you should always aim to use the freshest ingredients you can, it is even more important you do so when it comes to seafood. Get to know your fishmonger, not only will the produce you buy be of better value than supermarket offerings, but the taste will be far superior too. In this section there's a couple of personal dishes, including a recipe similar to the Spanish sardines I enjoyed on holiday with my late father, as well as pub classics like battered fish and chips plus my twist on fishcakes and moules marinières.

"Little fish" with cherry tomatoes, capers and a punchy lemon aioli

Preparation time: 5 minutes | Cooking time: 6 minutes | Serves 4 | gluten-free

A dish that will forever remind me of my late father. I was lucky enough to share a holiday in Spain with him just a few short months before he passed away. The "little fish" as he referred to them were plump sardines caught just off the Spanish coast; he ate them every day of that holiday and this is one dish that will always remind me of him.

6 tbsp mayonnaise

Sea salt

4 garlic cloves, finely diced

1 lemon, zest and juice

12x 60g sardines, scaled, gutted and gills removed

Olive oil

1 tsp smoked paprika

Black pepper

20 cherry tomatoes

25g unsalted butter

4 tsp capers

100g rocket

1 lemon, quartered

Preheat a grill to a medium high heat.

In a mixing bowl; combine the mayonnaise, a good pinch of sea salt, finely diced garlic, zest and juice of one lemon. Your lemon aioli is now ready to serve.

Lay the sardines evenly on a large flat baking tray that has been lined with foil.

Drizzle liberally with olive oil and season with the smoked paprika, sea salt and black pepper.

Place the cherry tomatoes around the baking tray and grill for 3 minutes. Flip the sardines over and grill for another 3 minutes.

Transfer the fish and tomatoes to a warm serving plate. Add the butter to the hot baking tray to melt then pour over the sardines and tomatoes.

Roughly chop the capers and scatter them over the sardines along with a good handful of rocket. Place dollops of the lemon aioli around the dish and serve with fresh lemon wedges.

Cod, chorizo and brie fishcakes with roasted red pepper purée

Preparation time: 2 hours 20 minutes | Cooking time: 15 minutes | Serves 6

This is a wonderful alternative fishcake adapted from the very popular salt cod fishcakes that adorn many good restaurant menus. We use chorizo to add saltiness as well as a subtle smoky flavour, which I think really elevates this dish.

2 Maris Piper potatoes

Olive oil

Salt and pepper

4 red peppers, deseeded and quartered

4 tbsp caster sugar

4 tbsp white wine vinegar

100ml passata

2 tbsp tomato paste

Saffron, small pinch

40g red onion, diced

200g chorizo, diced

500g cod fillet, skinned and boned

100g brie

1 egg yolk

30g fresh dill, chopped (reserve some for the garnish)

150g plain flour

3 whole eggs, beaten

300g fresh white breadcrumbs

Lemon, six wedges

Preheat the oven to 200°c/180°c fan.

Prick the potatoes several times with a fork and rub olive oil all over; season with salt and pepper and place directly onto the middle shelf of the oven. Bake for 1 hour 20 minutes.

Line a baking tray with foil. Place the deseeded and quartered red peppers on it, drizzle with olive oil and season. Cover with foil and roast with the potatoes for 30 minutes, then remove and allow to cool.

Once cooled, peel off the tough outer skin of the peppers and place the flesh in a food processor with the caster sugar, white wine vinegar, passata, tomato paste and saffron. Blend until it is smooth and velvety, then set aside ready to serve.

Remove the potatoes from the oven and allow to cool completely.

Heat up a drizzle of olive oil in a frying pan and sauté the red onions for 3 minutes until they start to caramelise, then add the diced chorizo and continue to cook with the onion for another 3 minutes.

Remove the onion and chorizo from the pan and allow to cool.

Make sure the cod fillet is free from any bones and dice into small pieces.

Cut each potato in half and, using a spoon, scoop out all the fluffy baked potato into a mixing bowl.

Break the brie into small chunks and combine with the potato along with the cooked chorizo, red onion, diced cod, egg yolk and chopped dill. Once mixed together, place in the fridge for 30 minutes to chill.

Preheat a deep fat fryer to 180°c or place enough oil in a wok or large saucepan to come halfway up.

Place over a medium heat and to test whether it's hot enough drop a cube of bread into the oil. It will be hot enough when the bread fries to a golden colour.

Remove the fishcake mix from the fridge and shape into 12 balls.

Dip each ball systematically into the plain flour, then the beaten egg and finally the breadcrumbs. Repeat this process twice with each fishcake.

Fry each fishcake in the deep fat fryer, wok or large saucepan for 4 minutes until golden brown and crispy. Remove from the oil carefully and place on a piece of kitchen towel.

Warm the red pepper sauce up over a medium heat and place a spoonful in the centre of a serving bowl.

Place two fishcakes on top and serve with a garnish of fresh dill and lemon.

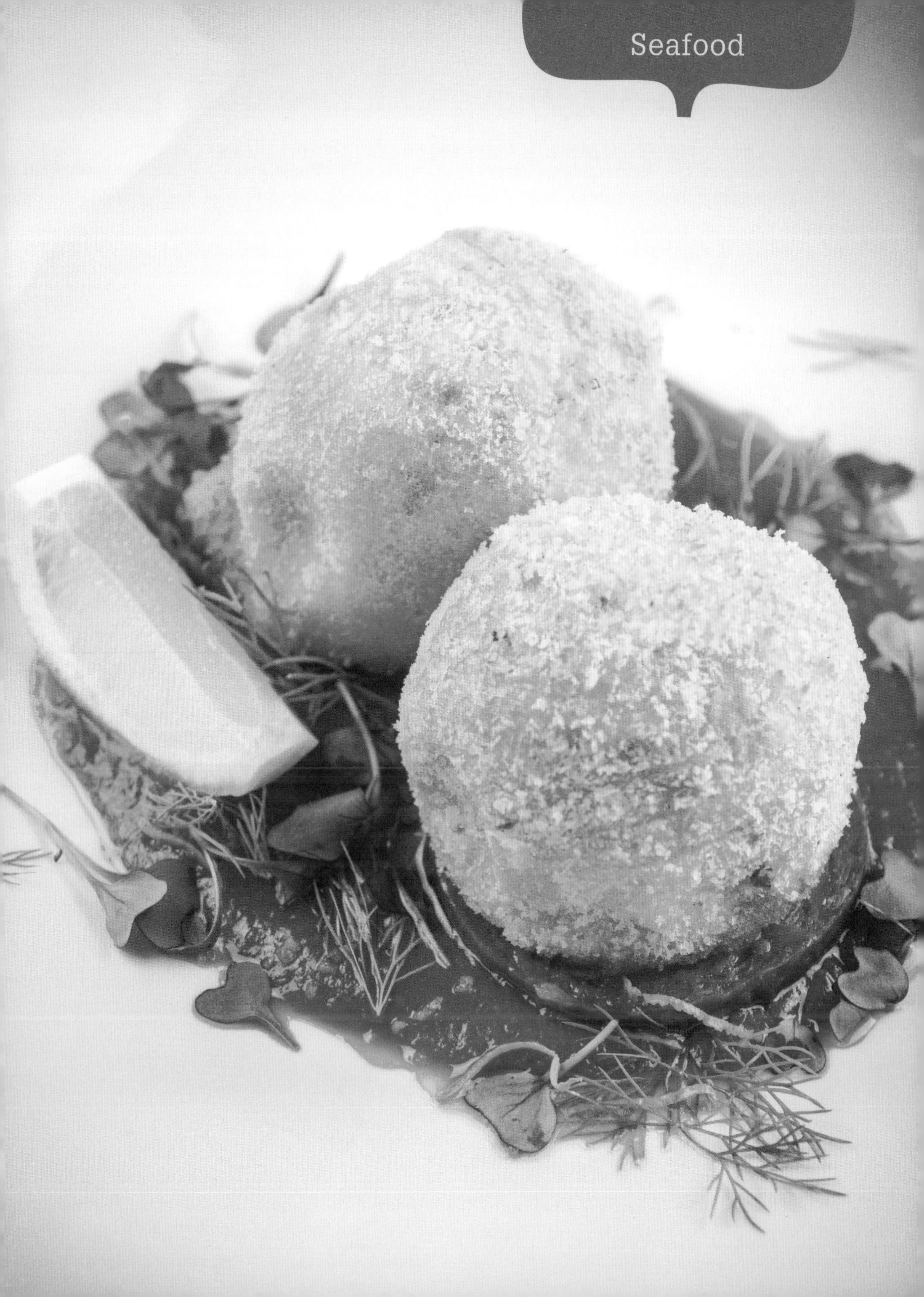

Crispy calamari with roast chilli, lime and tamarind dipping sauce

Preparation time: 20 minutes | Cooking time: 5 minutes | Serves 4

My mum loves calamari, so it's only right that I share my recipe for a very delicious version of a dish found everywhere these days. I've gone for a flour coating approach as I feel this gives it a better crunchy texture compared with batter, which I find can go a little soggy.

100g plain flour

50g panko breadcrumbs

1 tsp English mustard powder

1 tsp cayenne pepper

2 tsp fine salt

2 tsp ground white pepper

1 tsp turmeric powder

2 red chillies

Olive oil

1 lime, zest and juice

1 clove garlic, finely grated

1 tsp tamarind purée

2 tsp clear honey

2 tbsp light soy sauce

4 tbsp mirin wine

1 tsp fish sauce

4 prepared squid tubes and tentacles

50ml full fat milk

1 lime, quartered

Coriander, chopped

Preheat the oven to 200°c/180°c fan.

Preheat a deep fat fryer to 180°c or place enough oil in a wok or large saucepan to come halfway up the pan.

Place over a medium heat and to test whether it's hot enough drop a cube of bread into the oil. It will be hot enough when the bread fries to a golden colour.

In a bowl mix together the plain flour, panko breadcrumbs, English mustard powder, cayenne pepper, fine salt, ground white pepper and turmeric powder. This will become the coating for the calamari.

Wrap the red chillies in foil with a little bit of olive oil and roast for 15 minutes in the preheated oven.

Remove and allow to cool, then finely dice and place in a dipping sauce dish.

To the chillies add the lime zest and juice, garlic, tamarind purée, clear honey, light soy sauce, mirin wine and fish sauce. This is your dipping sauce.

Cut the prepared squid tubes into 1cm rings and slice the tentacles vertically into two pieces.

Dip the squid once into the milk and then into the seasoned flour, squeeze gently then shake off any excess flour.

Place the squid into the deep fat fryer, wok or frying pan and cook for 90 seconds until golden and crispy.

Pile the calamari high on a plate next to the dipping sauce and scatter the lime wedges around the calamari. Finish with chopped coriander and serve piping hot.

Fish and chips with tartar sauce and mushy peas

Preparation time: 20 minutes | Cooking time: 10 minutes | Serves 2

A truly British dish! When I think of fish and chips, I am immediately struck with a cold salty sea breeze and the chirping of seagulls. It's a unique dish in that wherever you are, it triggers a memory or a moment, which is why it's one of the nation's favourite. I use lager for my batter as the gas bubbles to create a crisp, light delicious finish.

200g plain flour, plus a little extra for dusting

1 tsp baking powder

250ml lager

Sea salt and black pepper

200g garden peas

20g unsalted butter

1 lemon, cut into four wedges

4 mint leaves, finely chopped

2x 250g fillets of sustainable white fish

2 portions of proper chips (see page 100)

Sarson's vinegar

Preheat a deep fat fryer to 180°c or place enough oil in a wok or large saucepan to come halfway up the pan.

Place over a medium heat and to test whether it's hot enough drop a cube of bread into the oil. It will be hot enough when the bread fries to a golden colour.

Begin by preparing the batter. Whisk together the plain flour and baking powder with the lager until you have a light batter the same consistency as double cream. Season with sea salt and black pepper.

Bring a medium sized pan of water to the boil and season with salt. Drop in the peas and cook until tender, this should take about 3 minutes. Drain and place back into the warm pan and add the butter, lemon juice squeezed from two wedges and the chopped mint leaves. Season with a little sea salt and black pepper then mash with a potato masher until you have your desired mushy peas texture. Place a lid on and set aside to keep warm.

Dust each fillet of fish with flour and then place in the batter. Very carefully lay into the hot oil, moving the fish away from you as you do this. Cook for 5 minutes until the batter is golden and crisp. It's best to flip the fish once during cooking to get an even cook and colour.

Carefully remove from the oil and straight away season with sea salt and place on a piece of kitchen paper to remove any excess oil.

Make the proper chips according to the recipe on page 100. Cook in the same hot oil for about 3 minutes until piping hot, golden and crispy.

Arrange the chips on a warm plate and season with a splash of Sarson's vinegar.

Add a big spoonful of the mushy peas and place your fish on top of these.

Finish the dish with a wedge of lemon.

Moules marinière with Parmesan and fresh red chilli

Preparation time: 5 minutes | Cooking time: 5 minutes | Serves 4

If you haven't yet tried mussels, you are in for a big treat with my version. I have used Parmesan and red chilli for an added kick, but if you're after a more classic style you can avoid using these ingredients.

2kg fresh mussels

2 garlic cloves, finely chopped

2 shallots, finely chopped

15g butter

4 bay leaves

100ml dry white wine

50g parsley, chopped

100ml double cream

50g Parmesan, shavings

1 red chilli, finely chopped

1 loaf crusty bread

Wash the mussels under a cold tap. Discard any shells that won't close when squeezed.

Remove any of the "beards" that can be found coming out of the shell.

Remove any barnacles that may have become stuck to the mussel shell with the back of a knife.

In a large heavy based saucepan sweat the garlic and shallots in butter with the bay leaves.

Add the mussels and dry white wine and turn up the heat to full. Cover and steam them open in their own juices for 4 minutes.

Halfway through this process, give the saucepan a good shake to make sure they cook evenly. Add the chopped parsley and double cream and bring to a simmer. Spoon the mussels with the sauce into four large serving bowls and top with Parmesan shavings and fresh red chilli.

Serve immediately with a good helping of crusty bread.

Seafood baked in a bag with fennel, celery, sultanas and cherry tomatoes

Preparation time: 10 minutes | Cooking time: 45 minutes | Serves 4

You will need baking parchment and tin foil | gluten-free | dairy-free

This is such a fun and easy dish to prepare and serve. It brings out the best in what seafood has to offer. Full of flavour and freshness.

16 new potatoes

4x 200g pieces of monkfish

100g fresh clams

8 king prawns, shell off, heads on

1 fennel bulb, quartered

24 cherry tomatoes, on the vine

4 tsp sultanas

100g samphire

1 red chilli, deseeded and chopped

2 lemons, halved

4 bay leaves

1 tsp saffron strands

4 springs of thyme

Sea salt and black pepper

200ml dry white wine

Preheat the oven to 200°c/180°c fan.

Bring a saucepan of water to the boil and season well with salt. Drop in the new potatoes and boil for 6 minutes.

Drain and set aside until ready to use.

Create the bags by tearing off 4 large 50 x 50cm pieces of foil and folding each one in half twice to make a sturdy, triple layered square. Fold the sides up slightly to make a shallow bowl and line this with a piece of baking parchment.

In each foil bowl place a piece of monkfish and then evenly distribute the clams, king prawns, fennel, cherry tomatoes, sultanas, the cooked new potatoes, samphire, red chilli, lemon (give them a little squeeze), bay leaves, saffron and finally thyme. Season well with salt and pepper and pour in 50ml of dry white wine into each bowl. Tightly scrunch and seal up the foil to make 4 parcels and place these on a baking tray.

Bake in the oven for 45 minutes, remove and place each bag directly onto a deep warm serving bowl. Carefully cut open with scissors and unfold each bag to serve. This dish is great with green beans or sprouting broccoli.

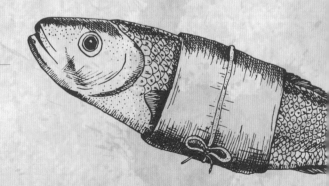

Smoked mackerel
with Jersey Royals and chives

Preparation time: 12 minutes | Cooking time: 12 minutes | Serves 6 | gluten-free

On colder nights, this warm smoked mackerel dish is a real winner. Developed originally as an item for the specials board at The White Hart, it soon became a popular choice and is now a regular feature on our winter menus.

150g Jersey Royal potatoes

10 smoked mackerel fillets

250ml double cream

1 tsp clear honey

200g strong cheddar cheese, grated

Chives, chopped

Black pepper

Sea salt

Preheat the oven to 200°c/180°c fan.

Bring a pan of water to the boil and add a few good pinches of sea salt. Carefully add in the Jersey Royal potatoes and cook for 10 minutes. Strain and set aside.

Remove the skin from the mackerel and break the flesh carefully in half length-ways; you should be able to pick out any small evasive bones that line up through the centre of the fillet.

Tear the mackerel meat into good sized chunks and place in a mixing bowl along with the double cream, honey, 100g of the cheddar cheese and chives.

Slice the warm Jersey Royal potatoes and add them to the mixing bowl, stir to combine all the ingredients.

Transfer this to either one medium baking dish or six individual dishes.

Scatter the remaining 100g of cheddar cheese over the dish and season well with sea salt and black pepper.

Bake for 10-12 minutes until bubbling and golden brown.

VEGETARIAN

Whether for health, religious, moral or environmental reasons, more and more people are choosing not to eat meat, or are trying to eat less of it. As a result chefs and restaurants are becoming more inventive with their vegetarian offerings – on The White Hart's menu dishes like pad Thai noodles with tofu or mushroom carbonara are just as popular as their carnivorous counterparts. Over the next few pages you'll find a selection of my favourite meat-free meals.

Butternut squash and goat's cheese lasagne

Preparation time: 30 minutes | Cooking time: 35 minutes | Serves 6

This has become a "go to" dish during my restaurant career. Such a wonderful pairing of flavours and textures, I've found that even people who aren't vegetarians opt for it, so I must be doing something right!

1 butternut squash, peeled and diced into large chunks

Olive oil

Salt and pepper

4 shallots, peeled and diced

3 garlic cloves, peeled and diced

10 basil leaves

150g Parmesan, grated

16 lasagne sheets

500ml passata

250ml double cream

300g goat's cheese, crumbled

Pine nuts, toasted

Preheat the oven to 200°c/180°c fan. Scatter the butternut squash on a baking tray and drizzle with plenty of olive oil. Season well with salt and pepper and roast on the middle shelf, uncovered, for 20-25 minutes until the squash has a little colour and is soft.

Heat a heavy based saucepan over a medium heat and add 1 tablespoon of olive oil. Add the shallots and garlic and sauté for 3-4 minutes until translucent and soft.

Add the butternut squash, basil and Parmesan to the shallots and stir well to create a semi smooth mixture.

Get a baking dish large enough to fit in four of the lasagne sheets along the bottom. Then begin assembling your lasagne. Add a little passata to the bottom of the dish then four of the lasagne sheets, then a third of the butternut squash filling, then a third of the passata, double cream and goat's cheese. Continue this process until you complete the last layer with a sprinkling of goat's cheese.

Drizzle with olive oil and season well. Bake in the preheated oven for 35 minutes until the top is golden and bubbling.

When you remove it from the oven, allow it to rest for 5 minutes while you prepare big chunks of bread or a lovely bowl of dressed leaves to enjoy this with. Scatter the lasagne with a generous handful of toasted pine nuts to really finish the dish off.

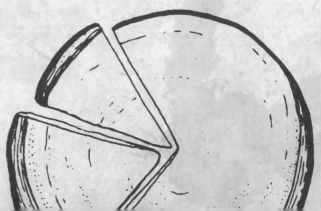

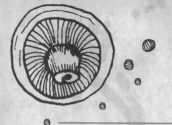

Creamy wild mushroom pie

Preparation time: 30 minutes | Cooking time: 30 minutes | Serves 6 | gluten-free

Mushrooms, garlic, cream... there's something about these wonderfully earthy and decadent ingredients that make it nearly impossible to dislike them, especially when combined together like this. I've found this meal has the ability to make even the most avid of meat eaters tell themselves: "I could go veggie!"

4 large portobello mushrooms

200g button mushrooms

200g mixed wild mushrooms

Olive oil

½ leek, sliced

6 shallots, diced

4 garlic cloves, crushed

1 stick celery, diced

10 sage leaves, chopped

50g salted butter

Sea salt and black pepper

300ml double cream

150g mascarpone cheese

50g parsley, chopped

Truffle oil

Creamy mash for 6, see page 99

100g cheddar cheese, grated

Preheat the oven to 240°c/220°c fan.

Begin by preparing the mushrooms. Wash them all thoroughly under a cold tap to get rid of excess dirt. Dice the large portobello mushrooms into big chunks and halve the button mushrooms. The wild mushrooms can be roughly chopped.

In a heavy-based pan, heat up a drizzle of olive oil over a medium to high heat and sauté the leek, shallots, garlic and celery for 5-10 minutes until soft and translucent.

Add the sage, along with all the mushrooms.

Add the butter and season generously with salt and pepper. Continue to cook the mushrooms over a medium heat for a further 10 minutes, stirring well, until they just begin to soften.

Add the double cream, mascarpone cheese and parsley to incorporate everything together. Add the mushroom mixture to a large baking dish and drizzle liberally with truffle oil.

Heat up the creamy mash if it has been prepared before and add the cheddar cheese to it. Either place this mixture into a piping bag and pipe on top of the mushroom mix or spoon it on and fluff up with a fork. Season the top with salt and pepper and drizzle with a little olive oil.

Bake in the preheated oven for 25 minutes until it's bubbly at the sides and golden on top. Let it sit for 5 minutes before serving as it will be extremely hot.

Pad Thai noodles with tofu

Preparation time: 10-15 minutes | Cooking time: 5-6 minutes | Serves 2 | gluten free

Thailand is a dream holiday of mine! I have not yet been lucky enough to visit and sample the authentic native dishes, but the flavours, freshness and vibrancy of their cuisine intrigues me so much. This is my version of a popular dish and the closest I've got to Thailand so far!

2 tsp tamarind paste

2 tsp rice wine vinegar

30g palm sugar, grated

2 limes

1 tsp fish sauce, optional

130g flat rice noodles

1 tsp sesame oil

3 tbsp groundnut oil

1 small red onion, sliced

1 clove garlic, sliced

1 red chilli, deseeded and sliced

4 spring onions, large slices

1 small carrot, fine julienne strips

1 egg, beaten

50g unsalted peanuts, shelled

20g Thai basil, chopped

100g firm tofu, cut into 2cm x 2cm chunks

80g bean sprouts

20g coriander, chopped

In a small bowl mix the tamarind paste, rice wine vinegar, palm sugar, the juice of one lime and the optional fish sauce. Stir until the sugar dissolves and set aside, this is the tamarind sauce.

Cook the noodles as per the cooking instructions on the packet and place into cold water to stop the cooking process. Drain and toss with the sesame oil.

Prepare the rest of the ingredients and have them in front of you.

Heat a large wok up with the groundnut oil until it's smoking hot. Make sure you turn your extractor fan on full and crack open a window!

When ready, quickly add the red onion, garlic, chilli, spring onions and carrot. Toss to keep the vegetables moving, and cook for 2 minutes. Remove using a slotted spoon and reserve on a plate. In the reserved oil add the beaten egg and cook for 1 minute until firm and scrambled. Add in the peanuts and Thai basil, then place back in the garlic and chilli mix. Toss well then add in the tofu, noodles, beansprouts and tamarind sauce. Continue to cook for another 3-4 minutes, tossing all the time to evenly cook and combine the flavours.

Divide the mixture between two warm bowls and top with a wedge of half a lime and chopped coriander.

Pearl barley, pumpkin and goats cheese risotto

Preparation time: 10 minutes plus 1 hour soaking | Cooking time: 40 minutes | Serves 6

Sometimes you can't beat a good risotto, but this particular one is a little bit different. I have always prepared our risottos with the highly underused pearl barley grain over risotto rice. It's amazing and has an awesome texture and nutty flavour. It's also a lot more forgiving than risotto rice, so it's a great ingredient to learn to cook with.

1 small pumpkin, skin and seeds removed, large dice

Olive oil

Sea salt and black pepper

6 shallots, diced

2 garlic cloves, diced

1 celery stick, diced

20g sage leaves, finely sliced

300g pearl barley, soaked in cold water for an hour, then rinsed and drained

1 litre vegetable stock (see page 159)

150g goat's cheese, crumbled

50g mascarpone cheese

50g parsley, finely chopped

50g toasted pine nuts

Preheat the oven to 180°c/160°c fan.

Lay the pumpkin on a baking tray and drizzle liberally with olive oil, season with sea salt and black pepper and roast, uncovered, on the middle shelf for 30-35 minutes until soft in texture.

In a heavy based saucepan heat up a drizzle of olive oil over a medium heat.

Add the shallots, garlic, celery and sage and sauté for 6 minutes until caramelised and they are starting to turn translucent.

Add the washed and drained pearl barley and stir well to combine.

Add the vegetable stock and bring the mixture to a simmer for 12-14 minutes. The barley should have soaked up the stock to become tender and plump.

Turn the heat down to low and add the goat's cheese, mascarpone, roast pumpkin and chopped parsley. Stir everything well a few times and heat through for another 3 minutes, then cover with a lid and allow to rest for 3 minutes.

To serve, place a large spoonful of risotto in the centre of a serving bowl and top with toasted pine nuts, a drizzle of olive oil and season with fresh black pepper and sea salt.

Wild mushroom and pea "carbonara"

Preparation time: 5 minutes | Cooking time: 10 minutes | Serves 2

While this may not the most traditional method, and it certainly bends a few rules, it's nonetheless a quick alternative, ideal for a mid-week dinner.

Olive oil

1 garlic clove, minced

50g unsalted butter

100g mixed wild mushrooms, torn and chopped roughly

Sea salt and black pepper

100ml white wine

100ml double cream

300g fresh tagliatelle

50g frozen peas

½ lemon, zest and juice

100g fresh Parmesan cheese, grated

1 whole large egg, beaten

Bring a large pan of water to a rolling boil, and add a good tablespoon of salt to it.

In a large deep-sided frying pan add a swig of olive oil and place over a medium heat.

Add the garlic and stir around the pan, then add in the butter and the wild mushrooms. Sauté for 3-4 minutes until the mushrooms are soft and juicy. Season well with sea salt and pepper.

Next add in the white wine and cook this out for another 2 minutes to reduce slightly. Then add in the double cream. Turn the heat down to low and let it simmer.

Add the pasta and peas to the pan of boiling water and cook for 4 minutes. Just before you drain the water, take a ladle of the water and add this to the mushroom cream sauce. Now drain the pasta and peas into a colander, shake well to get rid of excess and add this to the sauce.

Remove from the heat and add the zest and juice of the lemon, the Parmesan cheese and the beaten egg. Toss gently to incorporate everything.

The sauce should look rich and glossy.

Divide into warm bowls and finish each dish with a splash of olive oil and a good twist of freshly ground black pepper.

MEAT

There's nothing better than pub classics done well. From our barbaric burger to the perfectly peppered rib eye steak, tempting toad in the hole or traditional chicken and ham hock pie – this section is all about hearty British food that makes you feel all warm inside. I've also thrown in a couple of dishes from further afield, including my favourite beef curry – a Thai style panang – as well as a southern American fried chicken recipe.

The White Hart's 'Barbaric Burger'

Preparation time: 1 hour | Cooking time: 25 minutes | Serves 8

The origins of this burger stem back to a negative TripAdvisor review in which our house burger was described as being "barbaric". Seizing an opportunity, we decided to run with the name and make them bigger and better than ever. It is now the best selling main dish on the menu, with regular customers coming back just for a taste of the barbarity!

1.6kg minced beef, ask your butcher to have it not too lean

1 tsp English mustard

1 tsp tomato paste

1 oxo beef stock cube, crushed

4 sprigs of thyme, leaves stripped from the stalk

1 tsp sea salt

Black pepper

16 rashers streaky bacon

200g strong cheddar cheese, grated

8 brioche buns

1 baby gem lettuce, leaves removed and washed

4 beef tomatoes, sliced

1 small onion, sliced

4 large gherkins, sliced

Olive oil

In a large mixing bowl combine the minced beef, English mustard, tomato paste, oxo beef stock cube, thyme, sea salt and a grind of black pepper. Cover and rest in the fridge for 1 hour.

Preheat the oven to 230°c/210°c fan.

Lay the bacon on a baking tray lined with foil and bake in the oven for 10 minutes, turning halfway through after 5 minutes. Reserve the cooking fats. Set the bacon aside on a plate and keep the tray.

Remove the burger mix from the fridge and divide into 8 even balls. Press gently to form them into good thick burger shapes.

Heat a dry frying pan over a medium to high heat for about 5 minutes and put the extractor fans on high.

Give each burger a good coating of olive oil and fry on each side for 1 minute to form a good crust.

Continue this process until all the burgers have been sealed, then place them on the baking tray used for the bacon, and cook in the preheated oven for 8 minutes.

Remove from the oven and position two bits of bacon and an equal amount of cheese on each burger. Return to the oven for another 3 minutes.

Remove and allow to rest for a further 5 minutes. Use this time to cut each brioche bun in half and brush the tops with bacon fat, then place on the bottom shelf of the oven for 1 minute to warm through.

To assemble place the baby gem lettuce, two slices of tomato, sliced onions and gherkin in the brioche bun. Then carefully top with the rested burger.

A perfectly barbaric way to eat food.

BBQ pulled pork with my coleslaw and fried tortillas

Preparation time: 30 minutes | Cooking time: 5 hours | Serves 8

Pulled pork is everywhere these days, so it's only right that I jump on the proverbial bandwagon and show you my take on it. It's not hard to understand its popularity; you'll find this dish magnificently moreish!

2kg pork shoulder, skin removed	2 tsp mixed spice
120ml tomato ketchup	Salt and pepper
100ml white wine vinegar	3 large carrots, peeled and grated
2 limes, juice	¼ red cabbage, finely sliced
200g dark soft brown sugar	2 shallots, sliced
700ml coca cola	¼ celeriac, grated
5 tbsp English mustard	6 gherkins, grated
4 garlic cloves, chopped	6 tbsp mayonnaise
4 dried chipotle chillies, crushed	8 tortilla wraps
2 tsp smoked paprika	Coriander
Vegetable oil, for deep-frying	

Preheat the oven to 180°c/160°c fan.

Cut the pork shoulder into 6-8 large pieces and place in a mixing bowl.

Add 100ml of tomato ketchup, the white wine vinegar, lime juice, dark soft brown sugar, coca cola, 4 tablespoons of English mustard, garlic cloves, chipotle chillies, smoked paprika, mixed spice and season well with salt and pepper.

Wearing rubber gloves, get stuck in and mix everything together well; then transfer to a large deep baking dish or roasting tray. Cover with foil and roast on the bottom shelf of the oven for 5 hours. Be sure to check every hour that it isn't drying up. If you think it is, just top up with a little bit more coca cola or water.

While the pork shoulder is roasting, make the coleslaw.

In a large mixing bowl combine the carrots, cabbage, shallots, celeriac, gherkins, mayonnaise and the rest of the English mustard and tomato ketchup. Season with salt and pepper and transfer to a serving dish. Cover and set aside in the fridge until ready to serve.

Preheat a deep fat fryer to 180°c or place enough oil in a wok or large saucepan to come halfway up the pan.

Place over a medium heat and to test whether it's hot enough drop a cube of bread into the oil. It will be hot enough when the bread fries to a golden colour.

Remove the pork from the oven and strain off the juices into a serving jug (you've got a damn good BBQ sauce there). Using two forks pull apart and shred the meat. Pile high onto a serving board or deep bowl and cover with foil to keep warm.

Cut the tortilla wraps into six big wedges and fry in the hot oil until golden and crispy. Drain on kitchen paper and stack next to the pulled pork.

Serve with the coleslaw, the jug of BBQ sauce and plenty of fresh coriander torn on top.

Beef short rib panang curry

Preparation time: 20 minutes | Cooking time: 4-5 hours | Serves 4 | gluten free | dairy free

This is a little adaptation of one of my all-time favourite Thai-style curries. It's creamy, rich and has a good spicy kick.

1 tbsp vegetable oil

1 red onion, diced

1 green chilli, chopped

4 garlic cloves, peeled

1 carrot, diced

2 red peppers, deseeded and chopped

4 beef short ribs

2 tbsp Thai red curry paste

2 tbsp dark soft brown sugar

1 cinnamon stick

1 star anise

1 tsp fish sauce

1 lime, juice

500ml water

1 tin coconut milk

1 tbsp peanut butter

In a large heavy based saucepan heat the vegetable oil and sweat the onion, chilli, garlic, carrot and peppers over a medium to high heat for 5-10 minutes, until soft. Place in the beef short ribs and seal the meat on all sides until well browned. Add in the curry paste, sugar, cinnamon, star anise, fish sauce and lime juice.

Add in the water and cover with a lid. Reduce the heat down to low and simmer for 3-4 hours. Keep checking on it every 20 minutes or so, making sure the water doesn't dry up. If it is, just add another 50ml - 100ml more. This liquor will act as a concentrated curry stock.

After 3-4 hours the meat should be very tender. Remove the meat from the sauce and set aside to cool slightly.

Add the coconut milk and peanut butter and stir everything together, bring the sauce back up to a gentle simmer.

Remove the short rib from the bone, it should just slide out very easily, and dice the meat into good sized chunks. Place the meat back into the sauce.

Simmer for another 2 minutes and serve piping hot with fresh rice and flatbreads.

Beef Wellington with mushroom duxelles

Preparation time: 4 hours | Cooking time: 30 minutes | Serves 2

This is my all time favourite comfort food. If done correctly, you should end up with the most perfectly blushing piece of beef that just melts in your mouth. Don't make the mistake I once made though by leaving the cling film wrapped around the beef!

500g beef fillet

Olive oil

1 tbsp English mustard

250g chestnut or button mushrooms, cleaned

Sea salt and black pepper

1 sprig of thyme

4 slices of prosciutto ham

1 pack of all butter puff pastry, pre-rolled

Flour, for dusting

2 egg yolks, beaten with 1 tbsp olive oil and a pinch of sea salt

Creamy mash (see page 99)

Rub the beef fillet in olive oil.

Heat up a non stick frying pan over a medium-high heat, then sear the fillet on each side. This should take about 1 minute.

Transfer to a plate and using a pastry brush cover all over in English mustard, then leave to cool.

Wipe the pan clean and place back on a medium heat. In a food processor, blend the mushrooms with a good pinch of sea salt and pepper to make a rather smooth paste.

Place this in the hot pan with the thyme leaves and cook out all of the moisture from the mushrooms. This should take about 8 minutes. Transfer the mushroom duxelles to a plate and allow to cool.

Take 4-6 large cuts of cling film and overlap them to create a two wide and three deep layer of cling film.

Place the four pieces of prosciutto ham on the cling film and then spread generously with the mushroom duxelles. Move the beef fillet to the centre of this and then carefully roll up the cling film so that it wraps the prosciutto ham and mushroom duxelles around the beef.

Twist the ends of the cling film to create a sausage shaped parcel and keep rolling this forward until it's a tight even shaped cylinder. Transfer this to the fridge and chill for at least 3 hours.

Lay out the puff pastry on a lightly floured surface and remove the beef parcel from the cling film.

Brush the pastry with egg wash and place the wrapped beef fillet on this. Wrap the pastry around this beef fillet to create a neat parcel. Cut away any excess pastry and tuck in the edges.

Wrap in cling film and rest in the fridge for 30 minutes.

Preheat the oven to 200°c/180°c fan.

Remove the beef Wellington from the fridge and take off the cling film. Brush all over with egg wash and make score marks on the top. Season with sea salt and black pepper, then bake on the middle shelf for 18 minutes.

Remove from the oven and allow to rest for at least 10 minutes.

Cut the beef Wellington into 1 inch thick slices and serve.

This is great served with creamy mash (see page 99) and a red wine and Port sauce.

Slow roast breast of lamb
with roasted vegetables

Preparation time: 30 minutes | Cooking time: 6 hours | Serves 4 | gluten free | dairy free

Breast of lamb is a severely underused cut of meat, probably due to the fact it's not greatly accessible in supermarkets; with this in mind, a trip to the butchers will guarantee what you want. Make sure to ask for it boned and rolled.

The recipe calls for four breasts of lamb, which may be seem quite a lot, but the leftovers can be used in salads with gem lettuce and pomegranate seeds, or even in hot lamb and mint sauce sandwiches. Delicious!

Olive oil

8 banana shallots

2 sticks celery

2 beef tomatoes

4 rashers smoked streaky bacon

4 breasts of lamb, boned and rolled into one joint

1 tbsp tomato paste

1 tbsp English mustard

Sea salt and black pepper

1 sprig rosemary

1 cinnamon stick

2 cloves

2 star anise

500ml chicken stock

4 large carrots

4 parsnips

1 head of fennel

250ml red wine

1 tbsp redcurrant jelly

Preheat the oven to 160°c/140°c fan.

Place a large heavy based roasting tray directly onto the stove over a low-medium heat. Drizzle a generous amount of olive oil in the tray.

Peel and dice four banana shallots and add to the roasting tray. Dice the celery and tomatoes and add this into the tray with the shallots.

Slice the smoked bacon into strips and add this to the tray with the shallots, celery and tomatoes.

Place the lamb onto a clean surface and massage the tomato paste and mustard all over. Add the meat to the tray and season well with plenty of sea salt and black pepper. Add the rosemary, cinnamon, cloves and star anise to the tray.

Give the tray a shuffle and scrape any sticky bits free with a wooden spoon. Remove from the heat and add the chicken stock. Cover tightly with tin foil and place in the oven for 5½ hours.

An hour before it's done, prepare the carrots and parsnips by peeling them and cutting them into large fingers or big cube-like chunks. The fennel can be cut into half centimetre slices.

With about 30 minutes left of cooking time, remove the lamb from the oven and strain the juices into a saucepan. Carefully lift the lamb onto a warm serving dish and cover with foil. The lamb will continue to cook and rest during the last 30 minutes.

Into the roasting tray add the parsnips, carrots and fennel, then season once again with salt and pepper. Toss everything together and place back into the oven on the middle shelf.

Turn the temperature up to 180°c/160°c fan and roast the vegetables for 30-35 minutes. Turn and toss them every 10 minutes for an even cook.

Add the red wine to the saucepan with the lamb juices and bring to a simmer over a medium-high heat. Add the redcurrant jelly and whisk well to dissolve in the sauce.

Cut the lamb into slices and serve with piles of roasted vegetables and a good slosh of red wine sauce.

Buttermilk fried chicken

Preparation time: 10 minutes plus overnight to marinate | Cooking time: 15 minutes | Serves 2

Fried chicken is something I still get excited about; tender and juicy on the inside and light and crispy on the outside. If you prefer boneless chicken then feel free to substitute the legs and thighs for whole breasts. The chicken is also best prepared the day before you plan to serve it, in order for the marinade to really soak in.

4 pieces of chicken, on the bone (thighs and legs are perfect)

300ml buttermilk

2 garlic cloves, crushed

1 bay leaf

½ lemon, juice

6 peppercorns, crushed

2 tsp salt

200g plain flour

50g semolina

1 tsp ground white pepper

1 tsp cayenne pepper

1 tsp cumin seeds

1 tsp English mustard powder

In a large bowl add the chicken, buttermilk, garlic, bay leaf, lemon, peppercorns and 1 teaspoon of salt. Combine well and cover with cling film, place in the fridge and leave overnight.

Preheat a deep fat fryer to 190°c or place enough oil in a wok or large saucepan to come halfway up the pan.

Place over a medium heat and drop a cube of bread into the hot oil to test the temperature. It will be hot enough when the bread fries to a golden colour.

Mix all the dry ingredients together and remove the chicken from the fridge.

Place each piece of chicken into the flour mixture and coat well, squeezing and shaking the chicken to create a good coating.

Very carefully put the chicken into the hot oil and fry for 12-14 minutes. Remove from the oil and drain on kitchen paper.

Serve immediately while piping hot, with lashings of barbecue sauce (see page 156).

Chicken and ham hock pot pie

Preparation time: 5 hours | Cooking time: 15 minutes | Serves 6

The classic combination of chicken and ham is at its best in this hearty pie. I'd recommend cooking the ham hock the day before, if you can resist picking at it!

Olive oil	4 cloves garlic, crushed
1 celery stick, diced	3 sprigs of thyme
1 carrot, diced	1 leek, sliced and washed
1 ham hock	125ml dry white wine
3 cloves	1 tsp wholegrain mustard
Salt and pepper	500ml double cream
1 whole free-range chicken	2 egg yolks
1 onion, skin removed, quartered	1 pack pre-rolled puff pastry

For the ham hock, place a heavy based saucepan over a medium heat and add a little olive oil. Add the celery and carrot then sweat for 3 minutes. Add in the ham hock, cloves and season with salt and pepper. Add enough cold water to cover the ham and bring to a simmer. Skim away any residue that floats to the top.

Place a lid on and simmer for around 4 hours, the meat should fall from the bone when it is done.

Remove the hock and allow to cool completely.

Place the pan back on the heat and reduce the ham broth down until you have around 150ml of fresh ham stock left in the pan. Strain out the carrot and set aside.

Preheat the oven to 230°c/210°c fan. Place the whole chicken on a roasting tray and rub with olive oil. Stuff the insides with the onion and garlic, season the whole bird with salt, pepper and thyme.

Roast uncovered for 15 minutes then turn the heat down to 180°c/160°c fan.

Continue to cook for 1 hour, basting the bird every 10 minutes. Remove from the oven and allow to cool. Take the onion out of the chicken and roughly dice.

Remove the meats from their bones.

Place a heavy based saucepan over a medium heat. Add a little olive oil and sauté the leeks and onion for 5 minutes. Add the boneless cooked meats along with the reserved ham stock, white wine, wholegrain mustard and double cream.

Reduce the heat and simmer for 10 minutes until thick and silky.

Add the pie filling to a large pie dish and brush the edge of the dish with egg yolk.

Place over the filling and trim away any excess pastry. Score and brush the entire top with egg yolk and sprinkle with salt and pepper.

Bake in the middle of the oven for 10-15 minutes at 200°c/180°c fan.

Serve immediately and enjoy.

Peppered ribeye steak with wild mushrooms, bacon lardons, proper chips

Preparation time: 5-10 minutes | Cooking time: 15 minutes | Serves 4 | gluten free

Steak and chips doesn't really need much of an introduction, but we like to add a twist to this classic dish by using an Asian inspired mix of enoki, oyster, chestnut and shiitake mushrooms.

4x 240g ribeye steaks

Vegetable oil, for deep-frying

2 tbsp black peppercorns, crushed

1 tbsp red peppercorns, crushed

Sea salt

3 tbsp vegetable oil

1 tsp cayenne pepper

30g unsalted butter

4 garlic cloves, crushed

100g bacon lardons

500g mixed wild mushrooms

4 portions of proper chips (see page 100)

Remove the steaks from the fridge a good hour before you plan to serve them. This helps take the chill off them and allows a more even cook.

Preheat a deep fat fryer to 180°c or place enough oil in a wok or large saucepan to come halfway up the pan.

Place over a medium heat and to test whether it's hot enough drop a cube of bread into the oil. It will be hot enough when the bread fries to a golden colour.

Mix the crushed peppercorns together with a good pinch of sea salt, vegetable oil and the cayenne pepper.

Rub this pepper mix well into every steak on both sides.

Heat a heavy based frying pan over a high heat until the pan is smoking hot, make sure to have your windows open and the extractor fan on full.

Place each steak into the pan, making sure they are not touching each other as this will create steam.

Fry on each side for 3 minutes, a good crust should form on the steaks.

Turn the heat down to medium and add the butter and crushed garlic cloves.

Baste the steaks in the pan with the melted butter for 1 further minute.

Remove the steaks from the pan and place on a warm plate to rest for 10 minutes.

Leaving the juices in the pan, return to a medium heat and add the bacon lardons.

Fry for 2 minutes and then add the wild mushrooms.

Sauté the lardons and mushrooms together for 4 minutes.

Fry the proper chips in the preheated fryer, wok or pan for 4 minutes until golden brown and crispy. Season with salt and pepper.

To serve, place each steak on a warm plate with a healthy spoonful of the wild mushroom mix. Pour the steak resting juices back into the pan and scrape off any sticky bits. Pour this over the steaks and pile a few chips onto the plate as well.

Pork saltimbocca with butterbean and lemon mash

Preparation time: 15 minutes | Cooking time: 10 minutes | Serves 4 | gluten free

A lovely alternative dish for a chilly Sunday afternoon – although it's great any day of the week, of course! If you're not a fan of pork, this could easily be adapted with chicken or even beef steak. Have a play around and make it your own with different herbs and spices.

4 pork chops, boned

16 sage leaves

40g chopped parsley

Sea salt and black pepper

½ lemon, zest and juice

8 slices prosciutto ham

Olive oil

60g unsalted butter

100ml white wine

Seasonal greens

Butterbean mash for 4, see page 92

Take each pork chop and slice through the middle, stopping just short of the other side to allow you to butterfly out the piece of meat.

Place 4 sage leaves and a sprinkle of parsley onto each butterflied pork chop and season well with salt and pepper.

Add a bit of lemon zest to each piece and top with 2 slices of prosciutto ham.

Cover each pork chop with cling film and using either a meat tenderiser or a rolling pin, lightly bash each piece until about 1cm thick.

Remove the cling film and drizzle olive oil onto both sides of each pork chop.

Place a large frying pan or skillet over a medium to high heat. Depending on how large the pan is either cook one or two saltimboccas at a time.

Place each one prosciutto ham side down into the hot pan and cook for 2-3 minutes.

Turn each piece and add 15g of butter for each portion. Continue to cook and baste for 3 further minutes. Transfer to a warm serving plate and continue to cook each saltimbocca.

When finished, add the lemon juice and white wine to the pan, and scrape off any sticky bits. Bring to the boil and pour over the pork saltimboccas.

Serve each one with a good helping of butterbean mash and some seasonal greens.

Roast duck breast with sour cherry sauce and creamed cabbage

Preparation time: 10 minutes | Cooking time: 20 minutes | Serves 4 | gluten free | dairy free

This is a brilliant dish to serve during the festive months or alternatively, serve the duck cold and sliced with the sour cherry sauce as a great summertime picnic hamper option.

100ml merlot red wine

300ml Port

120g dried cherries

75g caster sugar

3 tbsp red wine vinegar

2 tbsp lemon juice

1 bay leaf

4 large duck breasts

Sea salt and pepper

4 sprigs of thyme

Creamed cabbage for 4, see page 94

Preheat the oven to 220°c/200°c fan.

In a heavy based saucepan add the red wine, Port, dried cherries, caster sugar, red wine vinegar, lemon juice and bay leaf.

Stir well and cook over a medium heat for 30-35 minutes. Try to keep it at a very gentle simmer.

Remove from the heat and keep warm.

Prepare the duck breasts by scoring the white fat in 1cm intervals at a diagonal pattern, turn the duck breast and do the same scores again to create a diamond effect on top.

Season well with sea salt and pepper.

Heat a non-stick pan over a medium high heat and place the duck breast skin side down into a dry pan.

Cook the duck breast for 6 minutes, tilting the pan toward you every minute and spooning out any excess fat. Add the sprigs of thyme to the pan.

After 6 minutes turn over the duck breast so it's skin side up and continue to cook for another 4 minutes. Transfer to a baking tray and bake in the preheated oven for 6 minutes.

Remove and allow to rest for 10 minutes.

Add your creamed cabbage to a heavy based saucepan, and over a medium to high heat, bring to a piping hot temperature. This should take around 6-7 minutes.

Spoon the creamed cabbage onto a warm plate and slice the duck into 4-5 pieces. Fan these around the creamed cabbage and spoon over the sour cherry sauce.

Steak and onion pot pie with Guinness and bay

Preparation time: 15 minutes | Cooking time: 4 hours 30 minutes | Serves 6

You just can't beat a proper pie – so I have decided to put two in this book! This one is a classic and a veteran of the pie world, using shortcrust pastry like we do at The White Hart.

1kg diced stewing beef	2 tbsp tomato paste
275g plain flour	4 tbsp HP sauce
15g English mustard powder	100ml red wine
Sea salt and black pepper	500ml Guinness
Vegetable oil	400ml beef stock
195g unsalted butter	10 bay leaves
1 large onion, diced	20 shallots, peeled
1 large carrot, peeled and diced	75ml cold water
1 stick celery, diced	2 egg yolks
2 portobello mushrooms, diced	Mashed potatoes (see page 99)

In a large mixing bowl add the stewing beef, 50g of plain flour, English mustard powder and season with salt and pepper.

Heat up a large saucepan over a medium high heat and add 5 tablespoons of vegetable oil and 50g of unsalted butter. When the butter begins to bubble, add in the seasoned stewing beef. Cook until the meat has a good colour all over, then transfer to a colander over a separate bowl.

Return the saucepan to the heat and turn it down to medium. Add another 20g of unsalted butter and sauté the onion, carrots, celery and portobello mushrooms for 10 minutes until soft. Make sure you stir well and scrape off any sticky bits from the bottom of the pan.

Add in the tomato paste, HP sauce and red wine. Continue to stir and scrape off any bits that are stuck to the pan.

Add in the sealed beef and then pour in the Guinness and beef stock. Place in the bay leaves and shallots, stir well and cover the saucepan. Turn down to a low heat and allow to cool and simmer for 3 hours. Be sure to check every 20 minutes to stir and make sure it isn't catching on the bottom of the pan.

Remove the lid after 3 hours and cook for a further 30 minutes to thicken the sauce.

For the pastry, sift the remaining flour in a mixing bowl and either grate in or cube the remaining butter into the flour. Work quickly and break the butter into the flour and once you have a breadcrumb-like consistency to it, then pour in the water and bring the dough together. Work it together on a floured surface for 1 minute, then wrap in cling film and chill in the fridge for 10 minutes.

Preheat the oven to 200°c/180°c fan.

Remove the pastry from the fridge and roll out on a floured surface until ½ cm thick. Transfer the pie mix to a large baking dish and brush the edge with egg yolk.

Lay over the pastry and cut away any excess, but leave a good 1cm overhang to seal in the goodness.

Create decorative leaves from the excess pastry and glaze the entire pie with egg yolk. Make a few holes on top using a knife or a pair of scissors.

Bake in the middle of the oven for 15-20 minutes until golden brown. Serve immediately – it's great with our mashed potatoes, see page 99 for the recipe.

Toad in the hole with onion gravy

Preparation time: 30 minutes | Cooking time: 30 minutes | Serves 6

My guilty pleasure and a very underrated dish! My first real memory of this is during primary school lunchtimes; it was usually followed by a plain sponge with strawberry jam and custard.

With this recipe, to keep things simple, measure out the plain flour, milk and eggs all to the same line on the measuring jug.

150ml plain flour	1 large white onion, sliced
150ml full fat milk	2 bay leaves
150ml eggs	600ml proper gravy (see page 158)
1 sprig of rosemary	Vegetable oil
12 pork and leek sausages	1 tbsp beef dripping or duck fat, optional
Olive oil	Salt and pepper

Preheat the oven to 240°c/220°c fan.

In a mixing bowl, whisk the flour and milk together to form a thick batter. Add each egg in one at a time until you have a smooth batter, it should be the same consistency of double cream. Strip the leaves from the rosemary stalk and add to the batter. Set aside in the fridge until ready to use.

Bring a medium sized saucepan full of water to a boil, season well with salt and carefully place the sausages in the water. Poach the sausages for 2 minutes then remove and place on a rack to cool. This process helps stop the sausages from burning on top when they're in the oven.

In a heavy based saucepan, heat a drizzle of olive oil over a medium heat. Add the sliced onion and bay leaves and sauté for 10-15 minutes until caramelised. Make sure to keep them moving so they do not burn.

Add your proper gravy to the onions and set aside.

In a 30 x 30cm roasting dish, add 8 tablespoons of vegetable oil and the optional beef dripping or duck fat. Place in the centre of the oven and let the oil heat up for 10 minutes until smoking hot.

Carefully remove and place the sausages into the hot oil, then pour over your batter and sprinkle with salt and pepper.

Place back in the oven, being careful not to burn yourself, and bake for 20-25 minutes. Remove from the oven and cut into six portions (two sausages each). Place each piece on a warm plate.

Place the onion gravy back onto the heat and bring to a simmer. Ladle over a generous helping of gravy onto the toad in the hole and serve.

My Dad's chilli con carne

Preparation time: 5 minutes | Cooking time: 20 minutes | Serves 4 | dairy free

To immortalise and honour my late father, here is a recipe for a dish that I have never truly been able to replicate. It must be said, it's not an original recipe of his. He was literally copying instructions from the back of a Colman's Hot Chilli Con Carne packet seasoning mix! Nevertheless, when he cooked it, it was the bomb. A few of my dad's cooking techniques differ slightly to the guidelines (I think this is what did the trick!) so I've also included them here.

1 tbsp vegetable oil

450g lean minced beef

1 large onion, crudely diced

5 garlic cloves, peeled and crushed

37g sachet Colman's Hot Chilli Con Carne seasoning

125ml cold water

1 tin 400g chopped tomatoes

1 tin 400g red kidney beans, drained

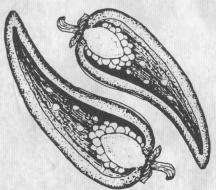

Place a large heavy based frying pan over a medium-high heat and add the vegetable oil. Brown off the mince in the hot frying pan with the onions and garlic. The onions should not become really soft, but rather just undercooked. Drain away nearly all off the excess fat, leave about 2 tablespoons in.

Add the Colman's Hot Chilli Con Carne mix to the cold water and add this to the mince, stir well then add the chopped tomatoes and drained kidney beans.

Place a lid over the saucepan and turn the heat down to medium, simmer for 10 minutes.

Remove the lid and continue to simmer for a further 10 minutes, stirring occasionally to make sure it doesn't catch. If you feel it's a little dry, just add a dash of water to loosen up.

Call your family from the kitchen to let them know it's ready and let everyone help themselves. It's great to serve with rice, in taco shells or even with garlic bread.

Bonus tip - if you have any leftover, try putting the chilli in toasted sandwiches with a little cheddar cheese! Honestly one of the greatest simple food pleasures ever.

SIDES DISHES

You can transform a meal with a decent side dish, whether that's creamed cabbage or honey mustard parsnips to accompany your roast, proper chips with your steak or French fries with your burger. I also think some of the sides I've included here are good enough to enjoy in their own right – try my cauliflower cheese for one!

Butterbean mash

Preparation time: 5 minutes | Cooking time: 10-12 minutes | Serves 4 | gluten free

This interesting side dish is a great way to utilise any tinned beans you may have knocking about at the back of the cupboard, just use the same process. Pair with grilled meats like chicken or pork.

Olive oil
10g unsalted butter
½ red chilli, deseeded and finely chopped
500g butterbeans, drained from brine

½ lemon, zest and juice
100g mascarpone cheese
Sea salt and pepper
40g parsley, washed and finely chopped

In a heavy based pan, heat up a swish of olive oil over a medium heat and add the butter. Sauté the chilli for a few seconds then add the butterbeans, lemon juice and zest, and mascarpone cheese. Cook for around 4 minutes, stirring well to make sure it doesn't stick.

Remove from the heat and crudely mash with a masher. Return to the heat and add about 50ml olive oil. Season well with salt and pepper, stir and cook for a further 3 minutes. Add the parsley and serve straight away.

Cauliflower cheese

Preparation time: 30 minutes | Cooking time: 30 minutes | Serves 6

Does it belong on a Sunday roast or doesn't it? It's up for debate. Personally I think it is a great addition to the table. My step father, Brian, on the other hand thinks it's a crime! Either way, it's a great dish even on its own with hunks of chunky bread and butter.

1 large cauliflower
50g parsley, washed and finely chopped

500ml cheese sauce (see page 157)
150g strong cheddar cheese, grated

Preheat the oven to 190°c/170°c fan and bring a large pan of water to a rolling boil and season really well with salt.

Remove the leaves from the cauliflower and carefully cut off each floret so they are the same size, then slice each in half. Carefully drop the cauliflower into the water and cook for 5 minutes until the tougher stem on the cauliflower is tender. Strain in a colander and spread onto a cooling rack to steam dry for 10 minutes. This just allows any excess water to run away or evaporate.

Place the cauliflower in a large bowl and add the parsley and cheese sauce. Mix all the ingredients together and place into a deep baking dish. Scatter the grated cheese over the top and bake in the preheated oven on the middle shelf for 25 minutes. The top should be golden brown and bubbly all over.

Allow to cool slightly for 5 minutes before serving as it's like molten lava straight away!

Creamed cabbage

Preparation time: 5-10 minutes | Cooking time: 25-30 minutes | Serves 4 | gluten free

This side dish is a complete contrast to the sticky red cabbage (see page 102). It's on the creamier spectrum of cooking and is great with poultry dishes or pork.

Olive oil	50ml white wine
½ white onion, sliced	450ml double cream
½ large savoy cabbage, sliced	Salt and pepper
100ml vegetable stock (see page 159)	1 tsp fresh nutmeg, grated

Place a heavy based pan over a medium heat and add a little olive oil. Sauté the onion for 5 minutes until soft and translucent.

Add the cabbage, vegetable stock and white wine. Place a lid on and cook for 10-15 minutes until the cabbage is soft and reduced in size.

Remove the lid and add the double cream. Give everything a good mix together and season well with salt and pepper.

Turn the heat up to medium-high and bring to a simmer. Add the nutmeg and cook for another 10 minutes until the cabbage and cream combine and thicken.

Serve in a warm dish with a little more nutmeg on top.

Dauphinoise potatoes

Preparation time: 20 minutes | Cooking time: 30 minutes | Serves 8 | gluten free

These creamy, garlicky potatoes make for a decadent side dish that will complement any Sunday roast.

600ml double cream
400ml full fat milk
4 garlic cloves, chopped
2 bay leaves
8 large King Edward potatoes

50g butter
100g Parmesan cheese
Cracked black pepper
Sea salt

Preheat the oven to 200°c/180°c fan. Add the double cream, milk, garlic and bay leaves to a large saucepan.

Peel the potatoes and slice them very thinly using a sharp knife or a mandoline slicer, aiming to get them around 3-4mm thick. Bring the cream mix to a simmer over a medium high heat and add the potatoes. Cook for 4 minutes then remove from the heat. Butter an oven proof dish and place the potatoes in it using a slotted spoon. Arrange them evenly so they slightly overlap each other and create multiple layers. Pour over the cream mixture so it just about covers the potatoes. Remove the bay leaves and sprinkle over the Parmesan cheese. Season well with sea salt and pepper and bake for 30 minutes until golden brown and bubbly.

French fries

Preparation time: 5 minutes | Cooking time: 10 minutes | Serves 4 | gluten free | dairy free

If you're not a fan of the thicker chip, these crispy French fries are the perfect alternative.

4 large Maris Piper potatoes   Sea salt

Preheat a deep fat fryer to 140°c. Peel the potatoes and cut into long thin French fry shapes. Half a centimetre thick or even a touch less is great.

Place these in a big bowl and run under a cold tap until the water runs clean. This washes off any excess starch that would prevent the chip from going extra crispy.

Pat the chips dry with a clean tea towel and fill up the fryer basket. Cook the chips for 6 minutes, shake off the oil and lay on some kitchen paper to remove any excess. You may have to fry the chips in batches depending on how big the fryer is. Once they have had their first blanch, turn the fryer up to 180°c and cook the chips until they are an amazing golden colour and super crispy. Drain on kitchen paper and season with plenty of sea salt.

Serve piping hot and with a large portion of barbecue sauce (see page 156).

Alternatively if you do not have a deep fat fryer, put 2-3 litres of vegetable oil in a deep heavy based saucepan and cook according to the instructions above. Make sure you are extremely careful as you do this.

Garlic roast new potatoes

Preparation time: 5 minutes | Cooking time: 25 minutes | Serves 4 | gluten free | dairy free

A great little recipe to use up any spare potatoes you may have! The recipe calls for new potatoes, but diced up Maris Pipers or good baking potatoes would work just as well.

300g new potatoes
Olive oil
1 red onion
1 bulb garlic

1 sprig rosemary
1 lemon, zest
Sea salt and black pepper

Preheat the oven to 200°c/180°c fan and bring a pan of salted water to the boil. Gently add the new potatoes and cook for 10 minutes. Strain into a colander and set aside while you prepare the onion.

Add a couple of good glugs of olive oil to a large heavy based baking dish, then place on the middle shelf of the oven. Remove the skin from the onion and dice into chunky 2cm pieces. Take the base of the garlic off and crush each clove with the flat part of a large knife, leave any hard-to-remove skins on though, just take away any excess.

Remove the baking dish from the oven and carefully add the potatoes, garlic and onion. Strip the rosemary from its stalk and sprinkle over along with the lemon zest. Season liberally with sea salt and black pepper and roast uncovered for 15 minutes. Be sure to give the potatoes a good stir halfway through cooking.

Serve immediately while they are piping hot. Great with any fish dish or even lamb!

Honey mustard roast parsnips

Preparation time: 5 minutes | Cooking time: 30 minutes | Serves 4 | gluten free | dairy free

Growing up I did not care for parsnips, I remember being asked to peel them and I thought they smelt so weird! These days I'll have them with near enough anything, but especially roast meats.

6 medium sized parsnips
3 tbsp runny honey
2 tbsp Demerara sugar
1 tbsp wholegrain mustard

1 tsp English mustard
1 tsp cider vinegar
1 tsp water
Sea salt and black pepper, to season

Preheat the oven to 180°c/160°c fan and bring a large pot of water to a rolling boil over a high heat. Season the water with a good tablespoon of salt.

Peel the parsnips and cut into quarters, removing most of the harder inside stem piece toward the stalk. Add them to the water and cook for 10 minutes.

Meanwhile add the rest of the ingredients to a saucepan and warm up over a medium heat for 1-2 minutes. Remove the parsnips from the water and place on a baking tray, allow the steam to escape from them for 5 minutes. Drizzle the honey mustard mixture over the parsnips, then season with salt and pepper and place in the oven. Roast for 12-14 minutes, turning and tossing halfway through cooking until they are sticky and well glazed. Transfer to a warm serving plate and enjoy.

The creamiest mashed potato

Preparation time: 5 minutes | Cooking time: 25 minutes | Serves 6

This method calls for a little bit more effort but it's more than worth it to guarantee no lumps and ensure a rich buttery flavour.

1.5kg Maris Piper potatoes, peeled and cut into 6 even pieces
100ml double cream

100g unsalted butter, cubed
1 tbsp salt

Put the potatoes in a large pan, top up with water and add the salt. Place over a high heat and bring to a rolling boil. Cook for 15 minutes and then strain into a large colander. Place back into the saucepan and mash well with a potato masher.

Next, add the potatoes a spoonful at a time to a fine sieve, pushing through back into a clean saucepan. Make sure you do it whilst they are piping hot – this may take a few minutes.

Once you have pushed all the potatoes through the sieve add the butter and double cream.

Place back over a low to medium heat and stir well to combine.

Serve immediately.

Proper chips

Preparation time: 5 minutes | Cooking time: 15 minutes | Serves 4 | gluten free | dairy free

The key to getting chips nice and crispy on the outside and fluffy in the middle is the potato you use. Maris Pipers or King Edwards are the go to for me.

4 large Maris Piper potatoes
Sea salt

Oil, for deep-frying

Preheat the deep fat fryer to 140°c. Peel the potatoes and cut into a thick chip shape, just bigger than 1X1cm is good.

Place the chips in a bowl and put under a cold tap until the water runs clean. This washes off any excess starch that would prevent the chip from going extra crispy. Pat dry the chips with a clean tea towel and fill up the fryer basket. Cook the chips for 10 minutes, shake off the oil and lay on a some kitchen paper. You may have to fry the chips in batches depending on how big your fryer is. Once they have had their first blanch, turn the fryer up to 180°c and cook the chips again until they are a golden colour and super crispy. Drain on kitchen paper and season with plenty of sea salt. Serve piping hot and with a large portion of homemade ketchup (see page 159).

Alternatively if you do not have a deep fat fryer, put 2-3 litres of vegetable oil in a deep heavy based saucepan and cook according to the instructions above. Make sure you are extremely careful as you do this.

Roast potatoes

Preparation time: 20 minutes | Cooking time: 1 hour | Serves 6 | gluten free | dairy free

I spent a good 15 years wishing I could make roasties like my dad, until I found out he had literally been taking them from a packet and placing them in some goose fat! Still, the key to it is having the fat hot before you put the potatoes into the oven. Try to avoid olive oil if you can as it has a pretty low burn point.

6 large Maris Piper potatoes, peeled and cut into 3 pieces.
5 tbsp goose fat

8 garlic cloves, skins removed and crushed
6 sprigs of thyme
Sea salt and cracked pepper

Preheat the oven 240°c/220°c fan. Place the potatoes in a heavy based pan of seasoned cold water over a high heat. Bring to the boil and let them cook for around 4 minutes. Turn the heat off and let the potatoes steep for another 4 minutes. Carefully strain into a colander and then spread them out onto a cooling rack to steam dry. This process allows any excess water to leave the potato giving you a lovely crisp coating; it should only take 10 minutes.

Meanwhile, add the goose fat to a large baking dish. Place in the oven to heat up for around 10 minutes. Remove the dish from the oven and very carefully, but with haste, place each potato into the hot fat. Season well with salt and pepper and scatter the garlic around the dish. Sprinkle with thyme leaves then place back in the oven and turn down to 190°c/170°c fan. Cook for 20 minutes, remove from the oven and carefully turn each potato over. Baste with the fat and cook for another 15-20 minutes. Serve straight away!

Sticky red cabbage

Preparation time: 15 minutes | Cooking time: 2 hours | Serves 6 | gluten free | dairy free

This dish is one that is slowly getting more popular, especially when combined with game or red meats. I'd also recommend trying it alongside other festive trimmings with your turkey Christmas dinner this year.

Olive oil

½ red onion, peeled and diced

2 cooking apples, peeled and diced

2 plums, pit removed and diced

50g dried apricots, diced

50g sultanas

Salt and pepper

½ large red cabbage, core removed and sliced

100g dark soft brown sugar

200ml Coca Cola

50ml red wine vinegar

5 bay leaves

2 star anise

4 cloves

1 cinnamon stick

In a heavy based saucepan, add a little olive oil and heat on a medium heat.

Add the onion and cook until soft, then add the apples, plums, apricots and sultanas. Cook for a further 3 minutes. Season with a good pinch of salt and pepper and then add all the other ingredients. Use a pair of tongs to mix everything up well. Place a lid on the pan and turn the heat up to high. Check the cabbage every 2-3 minutes to make sure it doesn't stick, stirring well whilst doing so. After about 15 minutes the apples should have broken down and there should be a lot more moisture in the pan.

Turn the heat down to medium-high and remove the lid.

Cook and reduce the cabbage by about half, this process should take about 1 hour to 1 hour 30 minutes. Be sure to check the mix is not sticking at all; if it is, turn the heat down a little and add a dash of water.

The cabbage should become almost jammy and sticky. This dish reheats really well in a microwave if there is any left over.

DESSERTS

I have a big sweet tooth so have included a whole range of desserts here to make sure everyone is catered for. Chocolate lovers will no doubt be drawn to the triple chocolate and pecan brownie or possibly the white chocolate cheesecake. For fruit fans I'd recommend the summer pudding or banana fritters, and for everyone else you simply can't go wrong with an Eton mess – the clue's in the name!

Banana fritters with sesame seeds and anise syrup

Preparation time: 5 minutes | Cooking time: 5 minutes | Serves 4 | dairy free

A staple of Thai cuisine and also many South-East Asian restaurants up and down the UK, banana fritters are hot, gooey and decadent.

Vegetable oil, for frying

100g self-raising flour

1 tsp bicarbonate of soda

2 tsp sesame seeds

1 tbsp caster sugar

1 tsp lime zest

150ml water, at room temperature

1 egg

4 tbsp honey

2 star anise

4 ripe bananas

Preheat a deep fat fryer to 180°c or place enough oil in a wok or large saucepan to come halfway up the pan.

Place over a medium heat and to test, drop a cube of bread into the hot oil, it will be hot enough when the bread fries to a golden colour.

Place the self-raising flour, bicarbonate of soda, half the sesame seeds, sugar and half of the lime zest in a bowl and make a well in the middle.

Whisk in the water to make a smooth batter, crack the egg into this batter and whisk again to incorporate fully. Cover with cling film and set aside.

Put the honey and star anise in a heavy based saucepan and place over a medium heat. Heat through until the honey begins to simmer. Remove from the heat and allow to come to room temperature.

Slice the bananas lengthways and then in half through the shortest part to create four even sized pieces per banana.

Dip each banana piece into the batter and fry for 3-4 minutes until golden brown. Remove from the oil with a slotted spoon and drain on some kitchen roll. Stack onto plates and drizzle with anise syrup then sprinkle with the remaining sesame seeds and lime zest.

Earl Grey panna cotta with lavender shortbread and fresh raspberries

Preparation time: 4 hours 10 minutes (including cooling time) | Cooking time: 20 minutes | Serves 6

A very quirky twist on tea and biscuits. We have substituted a small amount of the full fat milk for evaporated milk to really bring out a lovely malty flavour that goes so well with tea.

100g unsalted butter

50g caster sugar, plus extra for sprinkling

160g plain flour

1 tbsp lavender flowers

500ml full fat milk

100ml evaporated milk

60g caster sugar

6 Earl Grey teabags

3 sheets leaf gelatine

36 fresh raspberries

Preheat the oven to 190°c/170°c fan.

Beat the butter and 50g sugar together in a mixing bowl, until smooth.

Fold in the flour and lavender flowers to get a smooth and soft dough. Turn on to a work surface and gently roll out until the dough is 1cm thick.

Cut into 12 fingers and place onto a baking tray. Prick with a fork and sprinkle with caster sugar, chill and rest in the fridge for 20 minutes.

Bake in the oven for 15 minutes, or until a pale golden brown colour. Set aside to cool on a wire rack and store in an airtight container until ready to serve.

In a heavy based saucepan heat up the full fat milk, evaporated milk and 60g caster sugar over a medium high heat, stirring to dissolve the sugar until it just comes to the boil. Turn off the heat and add the tea bags. Allow to infuse for 20 minutes then remove the teabags, giving them a little squeeze to get the maximum flavour.

Place the gelatine sheets into a bowl of cold water for 5 minutes until they are soft and pliable.

Take them from the bowl and squeeze away any excess water, then gently stir into the warm milk and tea mixture until the gelatine fully dissolves.

Pour the mixture into six 100ml pudding moulds and place in the fridge to set for at least 4 hours.

To serve, fill a shallow dish with very hot water and submerge each panna cotta in for a few seconds to loosen up. Turn each one out onto the centre of a serving dish and garnish each with six fresh raspberries and two lavender biscuits.

Eton mess

Preparation time: 10 minutes | Serves 6 | gluten free

As a dessert that's not especially refined (there's a story that it originates from a dropped trifle!) the Eton Mess a great choice if you're ever in a rush and need a quick fix for a dinner party. Very minimal effort required, but big on fresh summery flavours.

750g fresh strawberries, hulled and quartered

½ lemon, juice

65g caster sugar

350ml double cream

6 meringue nests, broken

300ml good quality custard

½ lemon, juice

Take 150g of the strawberries, the lemon juice and 25g of caster sugar. Place them in a blender and blend until smooth to create a quick strawberry sauce.

Add the remaining sugar to the double cream in a mixing bowl and whisk until thick.

Layer all of the ingredients into six separate glasses, making sure to finish with a few juicy strawberries.

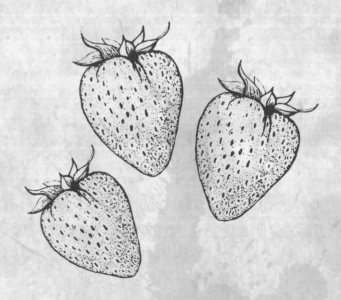

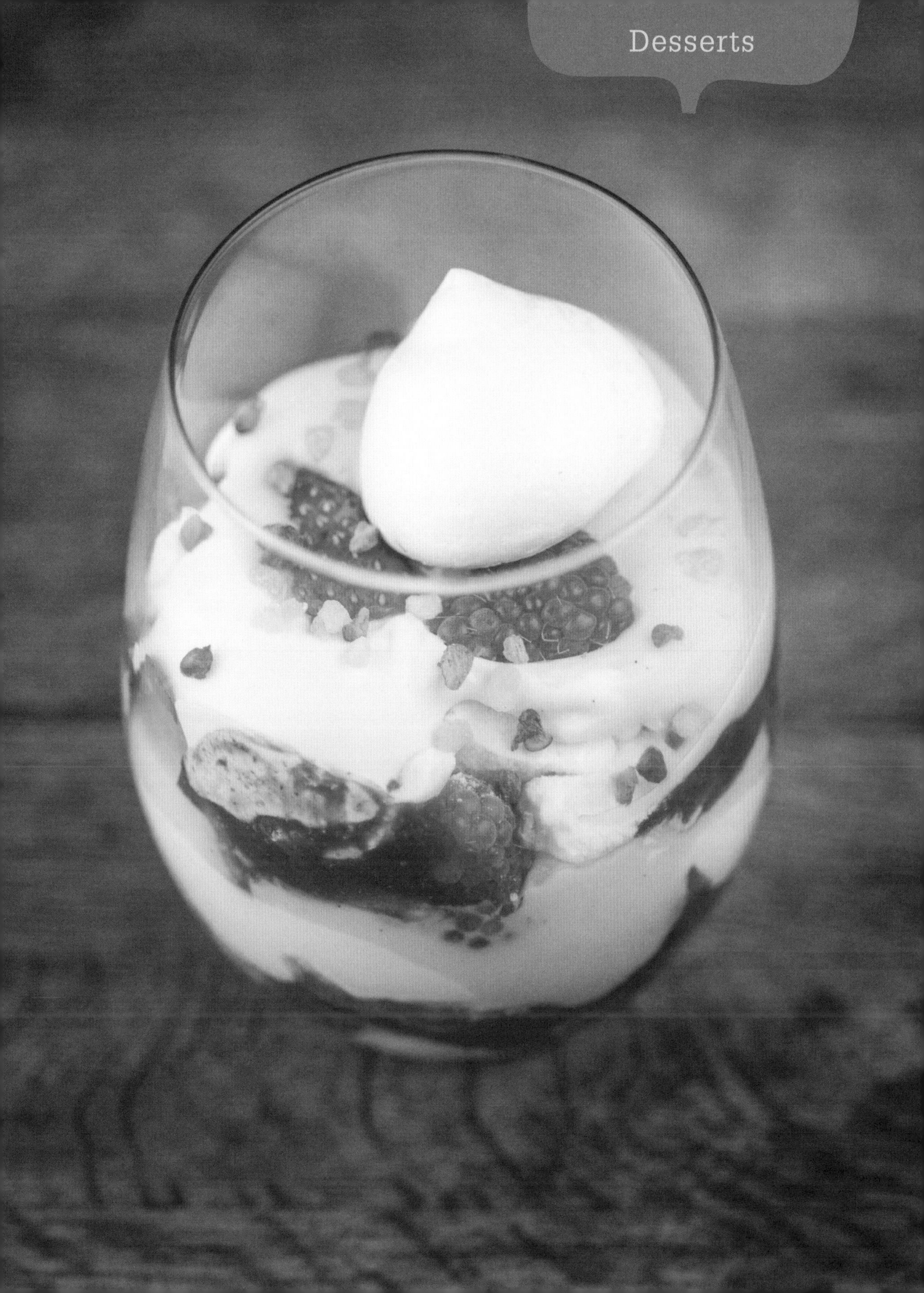

Fluffy pancakes
with bacon and maple syrup

Preparation time: 15 minutes | Cooking time: 10 minutes | Serves 2

6 rashers streaky bacon

150g plain flour

1 tsp baking powder

3 tbsp caster sugar

½ tsp salt

1 large egg, beaten

150ml full fat milk

2 tbsp olive oil

1 tsp vanilla bean paste

Unsalted butter

50g blueberries

Maple syrup

Begin by crisping up the bacon, Turn the grill on to high and line the grill tray with foil. Lay each rasher of bacon on the tray and grill for 4 minutes. Pour away any fat, turn the bacon over and grill again for another 4 minutes. Set aside until ready to serve.

Sift the flour, baking powder, sugar and salt into a mixing bowl.

In a jug, whisk the beaten egg and milk together; then whisk in the olive oil and vanilla bean paste.

Make a well in the flour mix and pour in the egg mixture. Beat with a fork until you have a smooth, lump-free batter.

Cover with cling film and allow to rest for 10 minutes.

Heat a non-stick frying pan up over a medium heat and add a knob of butter. Once it has melted, add a few ladles of the batter into the pan depending on how big you would like the pancakes to be. The size of a coaster is usually what I go for.

After a short while you'll see small bubbles appear on top of the pancake, this is your cue to flip them over with a spatula. Cook until both sides are golden brown and continue this process until all of the batter is gone.

Pile up with bacon sandwiched between each layer and give it a very generous douse of maple syrup. Finish by scattering with blueberries.

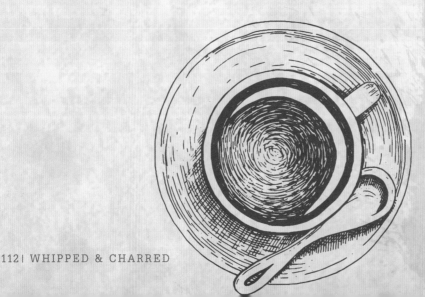

Honey semifreddo

Preparation time: 3 hours 20 minutes (including freezing time) | Cooking time: 15 minutes | Serves 8 | gluten free

This is an adaptation of a recipe a certain Nigella is responsible for. Honey is such an important ingredient worldwide. Not just for cooking with, it has huge benefits in medicine and has been used for hundreds, if not thousands of years to cure illness. Sadly the honeybee is under threat and it is vital we all do something to protect them. Support your local honey trade! There are beekeepers all around us who can provide you the most amazing raw honey.

1 whole large egg

5 large egg yolks

125ml clear honey

300ml double cream

½ lemon, juice

25g rice crispies

Line a terrine mould or bread loaf tin with cling film.

Place a large heatproof bowl over a pan of simmering water and add the whole egg, egg yolks and 100ml of the honey. Using a balloon whisk, beat well until the mixture is thick, pale and glossy. This can take up to 5-6 minutes. Remove from the heat and set aside for 10 minutes.

Whip the cream until thick and carefully fold in the egg mixture. Stir in the lemon juice and rice crispies.

Pour the mixture into the prepared mould and place in the freezer for 3 hours.

Remove from the mould and slice into thick portions. Finish by drizzling with the remaining honey.

The notorious white chocolate and milky way cheesecake

Preparation time: - 4 hours 30 minutes (including cooling time) | Cooking time: 15 minutes | Serves 10

I've totally lost count of the amount of these cheesecakes I have sold in the last three years. It is the only dish I have ever kept on my menus at The White Hart. Honestly, half of the reason for this is for my own safety, the backlash I would receive if it ever left isn't worth the risk! All jokes aside... this cheesecake recipe is now in print, so you can all make it for yourself.

400g digestive biscuits

150g butter, melted

150g white chocolate

10 milky way chocolate bars

350ml double cream

100g caster sugar

1 tsp vanilla paste

500g full fat cream cheese

500g mascarpone

Toffee popcorn, to serve

Fresh raspberries, to serve

Begin by making the biscuit base, break the digestive biscuits into a food processor and blitz until a fine crumb. Add in the melted butter and stir well to combine. Place equal amounts of the biscuit into ten individual ring moulds, or one large cake tin, and push down with the back of a spoon, making sure you get the biscuit to the edges and it's quite firm and compact.

Place the bases into the fridge while you prepare the filling.

Set a heatproof bowl over a pan of simmering water (making sure it isn't touching the water) and add the white chocolate and 5 of the milky ways. Heat through and stir until it has melted. Set aside to cool slightly.

In a mixing bowl add the double cream, sugar and vanilla paste. Whip either by hand or by using a mixer until it is thick and light. Gently fold in the white chocolate mix.

In a separate bowl, beat together the cream cheese and mascarpone. Fold this mixture into the cream and chocolate mixture until well combined.

Break the last of the milky way bars in and stir well until distributed evenly.

Remove the base(s) from the fridge and fill with the white chocolate cheesecake mixture. Smooth over with a palette knife and set in the fridge for at least 4 hours.

Remove from the mould using a blowtorch or a warm tea towel.

This dish is great served with piles of toffee popcorn and lots of fresh raspberries.

Strawberry shortbread with whipped cream and charred white chocolate

Preparation time: 40 minutes | Cooking time: 20 minutes | Serves 6

A simple showstopper. This dish is best enjoyed in the height of the British summer, when strawberries are ripe and bursting with juicy flavour.

150g unsalted butter

85g caster sugar, plus extra for sprinkling

240g plain flour

1 tsp freeze dried strawberry pieces

350ml double cream

40g icing sugar, sifted

1 tsp vanilla bean paste

500g ripe English strawberries

1 tbsp lemon juice

1 orange, zest

50g white chocolate buttons

1 tsp balsamic vinegar

Preheat the oven to 190°c/170°c fan.
Beat the butter and 75g caster sugar together in a mixing bowl, until smooth.
Fold in the flour and freeze dried strawberries until you get a smooth and soft dough. Turn on to a work surface and gently roll out until the dough is 1cm thick.
Cut into 12 equal discs and place onto a baking tray. Prick with a fork and sprinkle with caster sugar. Chill and rest in the fridge for 20 minutes.
Bake in the oven for 15 minutes, or until a pale golden brown colour. Set aside to cool on a wire rack and store in an airtight container until ready to serve.

Whip together the double cream, icing sugar and vanilla bean paste until you have a stiff but soft whipped cream. Transfer this to a piping bag.

Cut each strawberry lengthways into four pieces and place in a bowl with the lemon juice, orange zest and 10g of caster sugar. Mix well, cover and place in the fridge for 20 minutes.

Lay the white chocolate on a baking tray and using a blowtorch, gently char the outside. If you don't have a blowtorch to hand, place under a grill on a high heat for a few seconds. Allow to cool and break the chocolate up with a spoon or fork, then repeat the process once more. Crumble the chocolate up once cooled.

To assemble pipe a small amount of whipped cream onto a serving plate and pop a shortbread disk on top. Pipe a 1cm layer of cream onto this shortbread and then layer on slices of the strawberries. Repeat this process until you have two layers of cream and berries. Place the second shortbread on top. Add the balsamic vinegar to the juices left from the strawberries and spoon this around the plate. Finish with a sprinkle of burnt white chocolate.

Summer fruit crumble

Preparation time: 15-20 minutes | Cooking time: 35-40 minutes | Serves 8

Despite not even liking them as a child, these days I love a good crumble; they are perfect on a soggy winter's afternoon. If you ever have leftovers though, try them cold in a bowl with some Greek yoghurt for breakfast! It's an absolute winner.

100g strawberries

150g blueberries

150g blackberries

4 cooking apples

2 conference pears

1 vanilla pod, stripped of seeds (keep pod and seeds)

100g caster sugar

1 tbsp white wine vinegar

1 tsp table salt

100g plain flour

125g golden caster sugar (plus a little extra for dusting)

20g mixed spice

50g rolled oats

125g cold salted butter

Preheat your oven to 200°c/180°c fan.

Wash all of the fruit and drain well, shaking off any excess water. Remove and discard the leaves and stem from the strawberries then add them to a large mixing bowl with the blueberries and blackberries.

Peel, core and cut the apples and pears into inch-sized pieces and add these to the bowl of berries.

Add the vanilla pod and seeds, caster sugar, white wine vinegar and table salt to the fruit and stir together until the sugar starts to dissolve and a syrup is created. Cover this with cling film and set aside while you prepare the crumble top.

In another mixing bowl add the plain flour, golden caster sugar, mixed spice and rolled oats. Get the butter straight out of the fridge and either cube it up and add it the flour mix or grate it in.

Then, using clean hands begin to rub all the ingredients together for about 4-5 minutes until the mixture resembles breadcrumbs.

Add the fruit mixture to a large ovenproof baking dish then evenly distribute the crumble top over it all. Sprinkle with a little extra golden caster sugar and place in the middle of the preheated oven. Cook for 30-35 minutes until the top is beautifully golden brown and a jammy liquid can be seen bubbling away.

Set aside for 5 minutes to cool ever so slightly, use this time to arrange your bowls and warm up some custard... although I much prefer mine with ice cream!

Summer pudding

Preparation time: 6 hours 20 minutes (including cooling time) | Cooking time: 10 minutes
Serves 6 | dairy free - if not served with cream or ice cream

I wasn't a fan of summer pudding for so many years, and I have no idea why! It wasn't until recently when I indulged in a few homemade ones, that I became hooked.

200g raspberries

200g blackberries

100g blueberries

400g strawberries, hulled and halved

100g caster sugar

5 tbsp water

1 small loaf of white bread

Wash all of the fruit and place into a heavy based saucepan with the caster sugar and water. Cook over a medium heat for 5 minutes. Strain the fruit from the juice over a bowl and keep aside separately.

Line 6 small pudding moulds with cling film, leaving a little overhang so you can pull them out.

Cut the crusts from the bread and cut 4 of the slices into 3 short strips. Using a small circle cutter, and the remaining bread, cut 12 discs out.

Place 6 discs into the fruit juice and place in the bottom of each mould. Soak the strips, then line the walls of the moulds with them.

Spoon the fruit filling into each mould and then place the remaining discs on top after being soaked in the fruit juice.

Distribute any remaining juice over each pudding and gently push down to seal everything up.

Cover and chill in the fridge overnight or for at least 6 hours before serving. To serve, simply pull out the cling film and carefully remove the pudding.

Serve with clotted cream or ice cream.

Tarte tatin with dark rum and Chantilly cream

Preparation time: 10 minutes | Cooking time: 25 minutes | Serves 6

A classic French dish that we have not tried to mess around with too much – it's hard to change something so perfect! For different serving suggestions try ice cream, or if you're feeling decadent go for a spoonful of clotted cream.

200ml double cream

30g icing sugar, sifted

2 vanilla pods, halved lengthways and seeds removed

100g golden caster sugar

100ml dark rum

½ tsp ground cinnamon

6 pink lady apples, peeled, cored and quartered

50g unsalted butter, cubed

1 pack of all butter puff pastry, pre-rolled

For the Chantilly cream place the double cream, icing sugar and the vanilla seeds of one vanilla pod in a bowl and whip together until a stable but light consistency. Cover and place in the fridge until ready to serve.

Preheat the oven to 190°c/170°c fan.

Place an oven proof pan over a medium heat and add the golden caster sugar, dark rum, ground cinnamon, the remaining vanilla seeds and the pods. Shake the pan and let the sugar dissolve. Cook for 2-3 minutes until it creates a light caramel which is amber in colour.

Add the apples and stir everything together, continue to cook for a further 4-5 minutes. Add the cubed butter around the pan and then place over the sheet of puff pastry. Very quickly and very carefully tuck the pastry into the pan (do not use your hands! A Silicon spatula or spoon work perfectly).

Bake in the centre of the oven for 20 minutes or until it is golden brown and crisp on top.

Remove from the oven and get a serving plate much bigger than the pan to rest on top. Using an oven glove to grab the handle, very quickly and assertively, flip the pan upside down to release the tarte tatin. Be very careful of any caramel, a long sleeve shirt wouldn't go amiss!

Cut into six slices and serve with a very generous helping of Chantilly cream.

Treacle tart with orange and clove

Preparation time: 15-20 minutes | Cooking time: 1 hour 10 minutes | Makes one large tart, good for 10 hungry people

This is probably my favourite sweet treat; it's warm, gooey and full of bad stuff! A truly decadent dessert and an all-time great.

For the pastry

110g butter, chilled and diced

225g plain flour, plus extra for dusting

1 medium free-range egg, lightly beaten

5g fennel seeds

30g caster sugar

For the filling

450g golden syrup

85g fresh breadcrumbs

1 tsp ground ginger

3 cloves, crushed in a pestle and mortar

1 orange, juice and zest

Preheat the oven to 190°c/170°c fan.

In a mixing bowl, rub the butter into the flour with your fingers until it resembles fine breadcrumbs.

Mix in the egg with a knife, add the fennel seeds, then very carefully work on a clean, lightly dusted work surface to form a smooth pliable dough.

Use a splash of water if the mix is too dry, but do not allow the mix to become wet.

Roll the dough to a thickness of 50mm and use this to line a 23cm/9in loose-bottomed tart tin, prick the pastry all over with a fork and leave to rest in the fridge for about 30 minutes.

Line the pastry with parchment paper and weigh down with rice or ceramic baking beans.

Bake the pastry blind for 10-15 minutes, then remove the paper and rice/baking beans and return the pastry case to the oven for another 8-10 minutes until light golden brown.

Remove the pastry from the oven and turn it down to 180°c/160°c fan.

For the filling, mix together the golden syrup, breadcrumbs, ground ginger, crushed cloves, orange juice and zest in a bowl and pour into the pastry case. Return to the oven and bake for another 25-30 minutes.

The mixture should be firm and will have formed a slight crisp top.

Remove from the oven and allow to cool before serving warm.

We enjoy ours sprinkled with caster sugar and a big dollop of clotted cream.

Triple chocolate pecan brownies

Preparation time: 15 minutes | Cooking time: 25-30 minutes | Makes 12

If there is one chocolate dish to rule them all, then this is it. The chocolate brownie, with all of its variations, is the king of the chocolate world in my opinion. Warm, gooey, sweet, sticky and oh so moreish. Try serving it with a simple vanilla ice cream to really bring out the rich flavour of the brownie.

200g unsalted butter, cubed

200g 70% dark chocolate, chopped

4 large eggs

200g caster sugar

100g dark soft brown sugar

100g plain flour, sifted

60g cocoa powder

50g white chocolate, chopped

50g milk chocolate, chopped

50g pecans, chopped

30g sultanas

Preheat the oven to 180°c/160°c fan.

Place the unsalted butter and dark chocolate into a heatproof bowl and quarter fill a small saucepan with water. Set the bowl on top of this and place over a medium heat, making sure the bottom of the bowl is not touching the water.

Melt them together, stirring occasionally, then remove from the heat and allow to cool to room temperature.

In a food mixer, add the eggs, caster sugar and dark soft brown sugar to a mixing bowl and whisk on full power for 5-6 minutes until you have a thick and creamy mixture which has nearly doubled in size.

Pour the chocolate and butter mix into the egg mix and fold together gently, making sure you do not knock the air out of it.

Now add in the sifted flour and cocoa powder, folding it gently in until it's well incorporated.

Lastly stir in the white chocolate, milk chocolate, pecans and sultanas until distributed evenly.

Line a 25 x 25cm shallow tray with baking parchment and pour in the mixture, scraping the bowl clean. Tap gently on a firm surface to settle the mix, avoiding any unwanted air bubbles.

Place in the middle of the oven and bake for 25-30 minutes. Check the brownie after 25 minutes and if it is still a little loose, place back in the oven for another 5 minutes. The top of the brownies should have a sheen to it and flake with ease when disturbed.

Once it has cooked, remove from the oven and allow to cool completely in the tin.

Transfer from the tin and cut into 12 even squares. The brownie should be gooey and stick slightly to the knife, but not runny or oozing in any way.

You can serve warm by popping in a hot oven for a minute or two, or simply heating in the microwave for 20 seconds.

COCKTAILS

From fruity favourites like the strawberry daiquiri or passion fruit martini to a classic stirred-down old fashioned, boozy Long Island iced tea or seasonal favourite eggnog – a well-made cocktail is a thing of beauty!

This section is dedicated to my lovely partner in crime, Sarah, who's passion for mixology and perfumes is wonderful to watch.

Apple and thyme martini

Preparation time: 3-4 minutes | Serves 2

Apple and fresh thyme is a wonderful combination of flavours. It's a natural pairing that tastes good and smells even better. They perfume each other so well and elevate the other's flavour profiles. So what better way to enjoy them than in a cocktail?

100ml Bombay Sapphire gin

40ml apple juice

50ml apple schnapps

½ lime, juice

4 sprigs of thyme

4 apple slices

Ice cubes

Start by chilling two martini glasses by filling with ice cubes and topping up with water. Leave like this until ready to serve.

Add all the ingredients to a cocktail shaker except for 1 of the sprigs of thyme and half fill with ice cubes. Place on the lid and shake vigorously for 30 seconds.

Pour away the water and ice from the glass.

Double strain the cocktail before pouring into the glass.

Garnish each rim with 2 slices of fresh apple and a sprig of thyme.

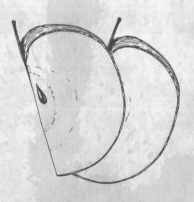

Bloody Mary

Preparation time: 3-4 minutes | Serves 1

Hungover? They say this is the drink to cure it! There are so many variations of this savoury creation out there but if you're looking for a little entertainment, get on the net and look at what they can do to this drink stateside. Whole burgers, lobsters and even pizzas can be found as a "garnish"… what is wrong with a stick of celery? This recipe follows a very traditional method. Simple and fantastic.

50ml vodka, William Chase is great

200ml tomato juice

3 dashes Worcestershire sauce

4 dashes Tabasco

½ tsp horseradish

Pinch of sea salt and pepper

Squeeze of lemon juice

Ice cubes

Celery stick

Gherkin

Add all of the ingredients except for the celery stick, to a shaker. Place on the lid and then carefully tilt the shaker from side to side for 30 seconds. Do not shake, as you will make the drink frothy, all you need to do here is combine them nicely.

Strain and pour into a long glass and top up with fresh ice. Garnish with the celery stick and gherkin and enjoy.

Eggnog

This one's perfect for those winter nights, especially during the festive season.

4 egg yolks

120g golden caster sugar (put a tablespoon to one side)

700ml full fat milk

300ml single cream

1 tsp fresh nutmeg, grated

50ml spiced dark rum

50ml bourbon

4 egg whites

In a clean mixing bowl, beat the egg yolks together with the golden caster sugar until thick and pale in colour; making sure the sugar is fully dissolved.

Add the milk, cream, nutmeg, rum and bourbon and stir to combine well.

In a separate bowl, beat the egg whites until they form soft peaks. Keep beating and gradually add in the reserved spoon of sugar. Beat until the egg whites form stiff peaks.

Gently whisk the egg whites into the milk mixture and chill well before serving.

Long Island iced tea

Preparation time: 3-4 minutes | Serves 1

This cocktail certainly packs a punch. Originally created by Robert Butt in the mid seventies, we've omitted the cointreau and used fresh orange juice instead, but you're more than welcome to add it back if you want it to be even more boozy!

15ml William Chase vodka

15ml Bombay Sapphire gin

15ml Sailor Jerry dark rum

15ml Jose Cuervo tequila

15ml fresh lime juice

15ml fresh orange juice

1 tsp sugar syrup

Diet cola, to top up

Lemon wedge, to garnish

Basil leaf, to garnish

Ice cubes

Place a cocktail stirrer in a long collins glass and fill to the top with ice cubes.

Pour over each measure of alcohol as well as the lime juice, orange juice and sugar syrup.

Slowly pour in the diet cola with one hand and gently mix together using the cocktail stirrer in the other hand.

Place the lemon wedge on the rim of the glass and rub all the way around then use as a garnish along with a single basil leaf.

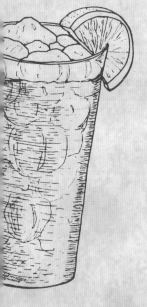

Mojito

Preparation time: 3-4 minutes | Serves 1

This is a traditional Cuban drink combining lime, mint, white rum and sugar. It's a true classic and wonderfully refreshing.

You will need a muddler and a tall glass

½ fresh lime, cut into four

2 tbsp caster sugar

10 mint leaves

50ml Barcardi carta blanca

Soda water

Crushed ice

Place the lime wedges into a glass, add the sugar and muddle (press down and twist half a turn) to release the lime juice.

Give the mint leaves a squish and rub with your fingers to release the aromas. Rub the mint leaves around the rim of the glass and place them in the glass with the lime.

Half fill the glass with crushed ice and pour in the Bacardi. Stir together until the sugar dissolves.

Top up with crushed ice, a splash of the soda water and finish the drink with a sprig of mint.

Old fashioned

Preparation time: 3-4 minutes | Serves 2

Developed in the 19th century, the old fashioned is a drink of sheer simplicity and class, made by muddling sugar with bitters and Scotch whisky. It seems easy but can be ruined with a lack of patience... so have some and watch magic happen.

1 sugar cube

4 dashes angostura bitters

1 tbsp hot water

Ice cubes

50ml good Scotch whisky

1 piece of orange peel

In a tumbler or rocks glass, place the sugar cube in the bottom and soak with the dashes of angostura bitters and the hot water.

Stir until the sugar has dissolved. Half fill the glass with ice cubes and add half of the whisky. Gently stir for 1 minute then add the rest of the whisky.

Hold the orange peel between your fingers and thumb and quickly bend it toward the top of the drink, this releases the oils from the orange and delicately scents the drink like a perfume would your skin. Place the peel in the drink and enjoy.

Passion fruit martini

Preparation time: 3-4 minutes | Serves 1

I adore all things passion fruit, but they're all the more better when paired with a good splash of vodka!

50ml cloudy apple juice

75ml vodka

75ml passoa (passion fruit liqueur)

1 tbsp lime juice

1 tbsp sugar syrup

1 egg white

1 passion fruit, halved

Add ice to a martini glass and top up with water. This will keep the glass chilled while you prepare your cocktail.

In a cocktail shaker, add all the ingredients (apart from half of the passion fruit) and fill up with cubed ice. Place the lid on and shake firmly and vigorously for about 25-30 seconds.

Pour the water and ice from the glass and strain the cocktail in. You should have a lovely meringue-like topping.

Place half a slice of the passion fruit on top for decoration and serve straight away.

Raspberry Bellini

The perfect way to use up a leftover bottle of prosecco in the fridge, our recipe is for a raspberry version, but it is done more traditionally with peaches.

150g raspberries
50ml sugar syrup
750ml prosecco

Add the raspberries and sugar syrup to a food processor and blend until smooth.
Strain and refrigerate until cold.
In a Collins glass, place equal amounts of raspberry syrup in each one.
Top up with prosecco and gently stir prior to serving.

Sidecar

Preparation time: 3-4 minutes | Serves 1

Though there's debate about whether this cocktail originated in London or Paris, it has remained timeless and is as popular today as it was nearly a hundred years ago.

50ml cognac

25ml cointreau

25ml lemon juice

Orange peel

Ice cubes

Place all of the ingredients into a cocktail shaker, with a good amount of ice cubes and shake vigorously for 30 seconds.

Strain into a coupette or martini style glass and serve with a lovely twist of orange peel.

Strawberry daiquiri

Preparation time: 3-4 minutes | Serves 1

I wrote my version of this recipe sat on a beach in Mexico. While the daquiri in my hand was probably a little different from the one you see here, it tasted fantastic.

The recipe calls for the use of a blender, but if you can't acquire one, replace the fresh strawberries with a good quality strawberry purée and shake the ingredients together in a shaker.

Ice cubes

50g fresh strawberries

50ml white rum

25ml triple sec

1 sugar cube

½ lime, juice

Crushed ice

Lime wedges, to garnish

Add 8 large ice cubes to the blender along with the fresh strawberries, rum, triple sec, sugar cube and lime juice. Pulse until smooth, but don't over-do it or it will melt quickly.

Pour into a chilled glass and top with some crushed ice and a wedge of lime.

The Bees Knees

Preparation time: 3-4 minutes | Serves 1

I stumbled across this incredible cocktail at The Experimental Cocktail Club in Chinatown, London. Nestled next to a wonderful American couple, Michelle and Andy, they told us about The Bees Knees and how it was a concoction from the prohibition era. A truly great cocktail and a wonderful night. Some recipes call for bitters and some don't, I prefer them in to just cut through the honey a little bit more.

50ml Boodles gin

25ml local clear honey

25ml fresh lemon juice

Couple of dashes of Angostura bitters

Ice cubes

Pour all the ingredients into a cocktail shaker and stir with a spoon until well combined. Top up with ice. Shake vigorously for 45 seconds and strain into chilled tumblers topped with fresh ice.

Whisky sour

Preparation time: 3-4 minutes | Serves 1

This cocktail is so simple yet so tasty. Even for the non-whisky drinker this is a hit. It's got a sweet shop element to it, a flavour combination that is reminiscent of the flying saucers and sour cherry sweets. A great cocktail for a beginner to master and impress your friends and family with.

50ml bourbon whisky

25ml lemon juice

25ml sugar syrup

1 egg white

Ice cubes

Orange zest or cherry, to garnish

Place all of the ingredients except for the garnish into a shaker and shake vigorously for 30 seconds. Getting the liquid ice cold is the key to a smooth drink.

Strain into a tumbler glass filled with ice and garnish with a little orange zest or even a cherry!

SAUCES

The backbone of most decent dishes; a homemade sauce will bring your cooking alive. While it may be tempting to pick up a packet version from the supermarket, try your hand at making your own ketchup, stock or mayonnaise. I guarantee more flavour with far less salt, fat and sugar content. Make them up in batches and store according to the recipe instructions. You'll never look back!

APPLE SAUCE

PREPARATION TIME: 4 MINUTES | GF | DF
COOKING TIME: 12-16 MINUTES | MAKES 1 SERVING
Deliciously sweet and great with pork, this simple recipe is a good way to get rid of any bruised apples you have in your pantry or have fallen from your trees.

2 large cooking apples, peeled and diced

3 tbsp caster sugar

1 tbsp white wine vinegar

1 sprig thyme

50ml water

Place all the ingredients into a saucepan and pop on a lid. Cook on a medium heat for 12-16 minutes, shaking and stirring the pan occasionally. Make sure to check that it isn't catching and burning. If you think it's getting a little dry, then just add a bit more water. Remove from the heat and check the apples are completely soft. Place the lid back on and give the apples a good shake to create the sauce.
Serve warm with anything pork! To store, transfer to a clean jam jar and keep in the fridge for up to 2 weeks.

BARBECUE SAUCE

PREPARATION TIME: 5 MINUTES | DF
COOKING TIME: 20-25 MINUTES | MAKES 500ML SAUCE
When I think of barbecue sauce, I'm thinking of the classic American barbecue scene. Racks of pork ribs, fried chicken and beef brisket. It's smoky, sweet, sticky and sumptuous.

400ml homemade ketchup (see page 159)

50ml Jack Daniels Whisky

50ml cider vinegar

200ml orange juice

50ml lemon juice

30ml Worcestershire sauce

50g dark soft brown sugar

2 tsp smoked paprika

2 tsp ground ginger

2 tsp ground white pepper

2 tsp mustard powder

Place all of the ingredients into a heavy based saucepan and heat up over a medium heat until it begins to simmer.
Reduce by half and funnel into clean sterile jars or bottles. Refrigerate and store for up to 2 months.

BEEF STOCK

PREPARATION TIME: 15 MINUTES | GF | DF
COOKING TIME: 6 HOURS | MAKES 800ML STOCK
If you've never tried your hand at making your own stock before, then this is a great recipe to get started with. I'd recommend freezing this stock into batches; it can be kept for 4-6 months.
To create a darker stock; try roasting the vegetables with the bones beforehand, you can ask your local butcher to cut them up for you.

2kg beef marrowbones, cut into pieces

1 tbsp olive oil

3 carrots, peeled diced

3 celery stalks, diced

2 onions, diced

2 bay leaves

8 whole black peppercorns

2 sprigs fresh thyme

1 sprig rosemary

1 tsp salt

2.6 litres cold water

Preheat the oven to 230°c/210°c fan.
Place the bones on a tray and roast on the middle shelf for 45 minutes. Turn and baste them every 10 minutes during this time.
While the bones are roasting, heat up the olive oil in a large heavy based saucepan. Add the carrots, celery and onion and sauté over a medium heat for 10 minutes. Keep the vegetables moving continuously and turn the heat very low.
Remove the bones from the oven and add to the saucepan with the vegetables. Place in all the remaining ingredients and top up with the cold water. Turn the heat back up to medium and bring to a simmer. Skim off any residue that floats to the top, turn the heat back down to low and loosely place a lid on top.
Simmer gently for 4 hours. The stock should be fragrant and light brown in colour.
Strain the stock into a large clean tub and allow to cool to room temperature before placing in the fridge for 1 hour.
Remove from the fridge and take off any fat that sits on the surface.
Use immediately or freeze into an ice cube tray for use later.

CHEESE SAUCE

PREPARATION TIME: 5 MINUTES
COOKING TIME: 10-15 MINUTES | MAKES 500ML SAUCE
This versatile recipe is the perfect base for cauliflower cheese (see page 93), lasagne or mac 'n' cheese, amongst many others.

100g unsalted butter

3 tbsp plain flour

400ml full fat milk

1 tbsp English mustard

150g strong cheddar, grated

In a heavy based saucepan, melt the butter over a medium to high heat until it's just starting to foam and smell a little nutty. Add the plain flour in and whisk well to remove any lumps. Turn the heat down to medium and gradually add in the milk until you have a thick smooth sauce, or what is known as a roux.
Turn the heat down to low and add in the mustard and cheddar cheese. Whisk well until it's all combined and the cheese has melted.
This is ready to serve or add to another dish.

CHICKEN STOCK

PREPARATION TIME: 15 MINUTES | GF | DF
COOKING TIME: 6 HOURS | MAKES 800ML STOCK
This stock uses the same principles as the beef stock recipe, but it is lighter in colour and flavour. It makes a good base for light broths and soup, especially when adding aromatics such as ginger and fresh chilli.

3kg chicken carcasses cut into pieces

1 tbsp olive oil

3 carrots, peeled diced

3 celery stalks, diced

10 chestnut mushrooms, sliced

2 onions, diced

2 bay leaves

6 sage leaves

8 whole black peppercorns

2 sprigs fresh thyme

6 parsley stalks

1 tsp salt

2.6 litres cold water

Preheat the oven to 210°c/190°c fan.
Place the bones on a tray and roast on the middle shelf for 45 minutes. Turn and baste them every 10 minutes during this time.
While the bones are roasting, heat up the olive oil in a large heavy based saucepan. Add the carrots, celery, mushrooms and onion and sauté over a medium heat for 10 minutes. Keep the vegetables moving continuously and turn the heat down to very low. Remove the bones from the oven and add to the saucepan with the vegetables. Place in all the remaining ingredients and top up with the cold water. Turn the heat back up to medium and bring to a simmer. Skim off any residue that floats to the top, turn the heat back down to low and loosely place a lid on top.
Simmer gently for 4 hours.
Strain the stock into a large clean tub and allow to cool to room temperature before placing in the fridge for 1 hour.
Remove from the fridge and take off any fat that sits on the surface.
Use immediately or freeze into an ice cube tray for use later.

MAYONNAISE

PREPARATION TIME: 2-3 MINUTES
COOKING TIME: 10-15 MINUTES | MAKES 500ML
Homemade mayonnaise beats anything you'll find on the supermarket shelf. It's richer, thicker and packs way more of a punch. It's also surprisingly easy to make, as long as you have a food processor! Trust me; unless you have arms of steel, this is not something you want to be attempting by hand.

3 free-range egg yolks

1 tsp Dijon mustard

200ml rapeseed oil

300ml vegetable oil

2 tbsp white wine vinegar

Sea salt

½ lemon, juice

Add the egg yolks and mustard to the food processor and turn on.
Combine the oils together in a large jug and then very slowly pour half of the oil into the food processor with the eggs. This should take about 5 minutes; it really does need patience! If you go too fast the mayonnaise won't emulsify and it will split.
After about half has been mixed in, add a spoonful of vinegar and carry on mixing until all of the oil has been used up. You should now have a very thick pale mayonnaise. Season well with sea salt, lemon juice and the rest of the vinegar if you think it needs it.
This will store for around a week in a sterile jar in the fridge.

MINT SAUCE

PREPARATION TIME: 5 MINUTES
COOKING TIME: 10 MINUTES (INFUSION TIME)
MAKES ENOUGH FOR 8 PEOPLE | GF | DF

Mint sauce is the perfect partner for lamb and this fresh and vibrant homemade version will transform a dish far more than any shop bought alternative. It also keeps well, so it is ideal to store in a jar for up to six months in the fridge.

1 large bunch of mint

1 tbsp capers

1 tbsp caster sugar

3 tbsp white wine vinegar

75ml boiling water

Strip the mint leaves from their stalks and chop very finely. Chop up the capers and add both to a bowl with the caster sugar and vinegar.
Pour over the boiling water and stir well. Allow to cool completely to infuse before serving.

PEPPERCORN SAUCE

PREPARATION TIME: 2 MINUTES
COOKING TIME: 20 MINUTES | MAKES 300ML, GOOD FOR 6-8 SERVINGS | GF

This is a sauce I can really get along with. After a solid decade of kitchen work, I still can't resist a bit of peppercorn sauce with whatever I have on hand to dip in it.

10g unsalted butter

1 tbsp cracked black peppercorns

1 tsp cracked pink peppercorns

1 tsp ground white pepper

25ml Port

50ml red wine

300ml beef stock (see page 156)

100ml double cream

In a heavy based saucepan add the butter and place over a medium high heat. Melt the butter until it begins to bubble and add all the peppers. Turn the heat down and cook for 1 minute, stirring to make sure it doesn't catch. Add the Port and red wine and bring to a simmer.
Now add the beef stock, bring back up to a simmer and reduce the liquid by half, this could take between 10-15 minutes.
Once reduced, add the double cream and bring back up to heat.
Serve straight away in a warmed jug.

PUNCHY AIOLI

PREPARATION TIME: 3 MINUTES (BEST DONE THE DAY BEFORE YOU WANT TO USE) | MAKES 500ML

AKA garlic mayo. I'm a sucker for aioli as it goes well with so many things; dip your chips in it, spread it on burgers or put it in sandwiches. By making it yourself, you can make it super punchy or tone it down a little to your taste.

1 batch of homemade mayonnaise (see page 157)

50g parsley, washed and finely chopped

Cracked black pepper

8 garlic cloves

Put the mayonnaise in a mixing bowl and add the parsley and a good few pinches of pepper. Using a zester or fine grater, grate the garlic and add that to the mayonnaise.
Stir well, cover and let it infuse overnight in a fridge before serving.
It will keep well for about a week in a sterile clean jar in the fridge.

PROPER GRAVY

PREPARATION TIME: 5 MINUTES | DF
COOKING TIME: 10-15 MINUTES | MAKES 500ML

Really this recipe is only plausible if you've done a full roast dinner and have a tray full of veggies and resting juices from the meat.

1 tray of freshly roasted vegetables, such as carrots, onion, celery and swede

2 tbsp plain flour

75ml red wine

500ml beef or chicken stock (see page 156 or 157)

2 bay leaves

Resting juices from roast meat

Get your tray of roasted vegetables and pour off any excess fats and oils that may be left over from roasting. Save these fats though as they are great for roasting potatoes in next time!
Place the tray directly onto the stove and turn on the heat to medium. Add the plain flour to the vegetables and stir well using a wooden spoon. You'll see it will start to stick slightly to the tray, this is your cue to add the red wine. Add the wine and whilst holding the tray with an oven glove; scrape off all the sticky bits from the bottom of the pan. Next add the stock of your choice, bay leaves and the resting juices from the meat.
Simmer in the tray for 10 minutes until the vegetables become extra soft.
Place a sieve over a large pan and carefully pour in the gravy. Now, using the back of your wooden spoon, push all the roasted vegetables through the sieve.
Place this pan onto a medium heat and bring to a simmer. Serve in a large warm jug and enjoy.

SUNDRIED TOMATO AND OLIVE TAPENADE
PREPARATION TIME: 10 MINUTES
MAKES 1 BATCH | GF | DF
While the traditional use of this condiment is spread over fresh breads such as ciabatta, sourdough or flat breads, you can also use it to add complexity to dishes. For instance try stuffing it into poultry or toss with fresh pasta.

150g sundried tomatoes

200g pitted black olives

6 anchovies

10g chopped parsley

1 tbsp capers

1 lemon, zest and juice

125ml olive oil

Place all of the ingredients into a food processor and pulse until you get a rough but well combined consistency. Enjoy immediately or store in a clean jam jar for up to a week.

TOMATO KETCHUP
PREPARATION TIME: 15-20 MINUTES
COOKING TIME: 1 HOUR | GF | DF
There's something about good quality homemade ketchup that'll trump the bottled stuff any day.

1 red onion, diced

1 stick of celery, diced

1 bulb of fennel, chopped

4 cloves of garlic

2 red peppers, deseeded and chopped

½ red chilli, deseeded and chopped

Olive oil

1 tbsp mustard seeds

5 cloves

1 tsp salt

1 tsp black pepper

1kg super ripe red, orange or yellow tomatoes, dice

(Or 500g fresh tomatoes and 500g good quality tinned plum tomatoes)

300ml water

50g basil

80g dark soft brown sugar

40ml lemon juice

180ml red wine vinegar

Place the onion, celery, fennel, garlic, peppers and chilli in a large heavy based saucepan and add a good lashing of olive oil. Add the mustard seeds and cloves. Begin to soften the vegetables on a medium heat. Season with the salt and black pepper.

After about 15 minutes add the tomatoes and water. Bring this mixture up to a simmer and reduce by half. Be sure to stir frequently.
Add the basil leaves and blend with a food processor until silky smooth, strain this through a sieve into a clean pan.
Add the sugar, lemon juice and vinegar and place back on a medium heat. Thicken until it's the consistency you desire.
Funnel the ketchup in clean sterile bottles and seal well. They should keep for up to 4 months in the fridge or a cool dark place.

VEGETABLE STOCK
PREPARATION TIME: 10 MINUTES | GF | DF
COOKING TIME: 30-35 MINUTES | MAKES 800ML STOCK

Olive oil

½ white onion, diced

½ leek, diced

1 carrot, diced

½ bulb fennel, diced

1 litre cold water

4 garlic cloves, crushed

4 tomatoes, diced

5 chestnut mushrooms, sliced

1 stick celery, diced

4 parsley stalks

1 bay leaf

1 sprig of thyme

15 whole black peppercorns

Place a heavy based pan on a medium heat and add a dash of olive oil. Sauté the onion, leek, carrot and fennel. Soften slightly by cooking for about 4 minutes.
Add the cold water and turn the heat up to high.
Add the garlic, tomatoes, mushrooms, celery, parsley stalks, bay, thyme and peppercorns and stir well.
Bring to a simmer and cook for 20 minutes.
Pass the stock through a sieve and refrigerate. Can be kept for up to 3 days or frozen in ice cube trays to be used later.

I wouldn't be here and able to do this book without many great people, I can't name them all but I'll give it a good go.

My inspirational grandparents Mama and Bampa, my incredibly supportive and hard-working mum Mandy, who deserves the world and more for being full of love and care for everyone around her. My step dad, Brian, who has helped mould me into a man; I cannot thank you enough. Both my awesome brothers, Ashton and Luke. My better half, Sarah, who has kept some sanity in me. My many aunties, uncles and amazing cousins, with special thanks to aunty Angie and my cousin Charlotte for being so extremely supportive and my biggest fans. The many chefs, waiting staff and KPs I've had the pleasure of working with; Mat Tucker, Richard Lenik, The Poffel Brothers and many more. Jules Kirby, who has been a great friend and colleague for the last six years. All my friends and loyal customers; Jack Milner, Richard Young and Rachael Kean, Karen and Jan, Judy and Anne, Jed Riddy, Jordan Denley and all the lads that are in every week.

Lastly, one final mention to my late father, Ian Curtis. Not a single day goes by when I don't think of you. You were always and continue to be here for me. Wherever you are and whatever you're doing, please know I have always been proud to be your son and I love you with everything I have.

Love Thomas x